LOVE'S LABOUR'S LOST

LOVE'S LABOUR'S LOST

William Shakespeare

WORDSWORTH CLASSICS

The paper in this book is produced from pure wood
pulp, without the use of chlorine or any other substance
harmful to the environment. The energy used in its
production consists almost entirely of hydroelectricity
and heat generated from waste materials, thereby
conserving fossil fuels and contributing little to the
greenhouse effect.

This edition published 1995 by
Wordsworth Editions Limited
Cumberland House, Crib Street, Ware,
Hertfordshire SG12 9ET

ISBN 1 85326 259 5

Printed and bound in Denmark by Nørhaven
Typeset in the UK by R & B Creative Services Ltd

INTRODUCTION

Love's Labour's Lost was first performed *c*. 1594. The text of the 1623 Folio is based on that of a Quarto edition published in 1598. A precise source has not been determined, and it may be that this is one of the few plays whose story Shakespeare invented.

Having forsworn the company of women for three years, Ferdinand, King of Navarre, and his three lords, Berowne, Dumain and Longaville, are sorely tried and eventually overcome by the embassy of the Princess of France with her three ladies, Rosaline, Katharine and Maria. The complications are wittily prolonged and the language the most ornate that Shakespeare wrote. This is a play that has been understandably called Mozartian, through *Lyly's Euphues* and the fashion it created was the immediate influence and the object of Shakespeare's affectionate satire. The extravagant conceits of the courtly lovers are a feature of the play, but Shakespeare has also created a gallery of minor characters, the fantastical Spaniard Armado, the pedantic schoolteacher Holofernes, Dull the constable and Costard the clown being the most notable. They are the kind that Ben Jonson would later develop into 'humours'.

Details of Shakespeare's early life are scanty. He was the son of a prosperous merchant of Stratford-upon-Avon, and tradition has it that he was born on 23rd April 1564; records show that he was baptised three days later. It is likely that he attended the local grammar school, but he had no university education. Of his early career there is no record, though John Aubrey states that he was, for a time, a country schoolmaster. How he became involved with the stage is equally uncertain, but he was sufficiently established as a playwright by 1592 to be criticised in print. He was a leading member of the Lord Chamberlain's Company, which became the King's men on the accession of James I in 1603. Shakespeare married Anne Hathaway in 1582, by whom he had two daughters and a son, Hamnet, who died in childhood. Towards the end of his life he loosened his ties with London and retired to New Place, his substantial property in Stratford that he had bought in 1597. He died on 23rd April 1616 aged 52, and is buried in Holy Trinity Church, Stratford.

Further reading:

R Berman: *A Reader's Guide to Shakespeare's Plays* 1973
B O Bonazza: *Shakespeare's Early Comedies: A Structural Analysis* 1966
B Evans: *Shakespeare's Comedies* 1962
A Leggatt: *Shakespeare's Comedy of Love* 1974
P G Phialas: *Shakespeare's Romantic Comedies* 1966

The scene: the royal park in Navarre

CHARACTERS IN THE PLAY

FERDINAND, *King of Navarre*

BEROWNE ⎫
LONGAVILLE ⎬ *young lords, attending on the King*
DUMAINE ⎭

BOYET, *an elderly lord, attending on the Princess of France*
MERCADÉ, *a messenger*
DON ADRIANO DE ARMADO, *a fantastical Spaniard*
SIR NATHANIEL, *a curate*
HOLOFERNES, *a schoolmaster*
DULL, *a constable*
COSTARD, *a clown*
MOTH, *page to Armado*
A Forester
THE PRINCESS OF FRANCE

ROSALINE ⎫
KATHARINE ⎬ *ladies, attending on the Princess*
MARIA ⎭

JAQUENETTA, *a country wench*

Officers and others, attendant on the King and the Princess

LOVE'S LABOUR'S LOST

LOVE'S LABOUR'S LOST

[I. I.] *The Park of Ferdinand, King of Navarre, hard by
the gates leading to the palace; trees and a coppice*

The KING, BEROWNE, LONGAVILLE, and DUMAINE

King. Let fame, that all hunt after in their lives,
Live regist'red upon our brazen tombs,
And then grace us, in the disgrace of death;
When, spite of cormorant devouring Time,
Th'endeavour of this present breath may buy
That honour which shall bate his scythe's keen edge,
And make us heirs of all eternity.
Therefore, brave conquerors—for so you are
That war against your own affections
And the huge army of the world's desires—   10
Our late edict shall strongly stand in force:
Navarre shall be the wonder of the world,
Our court shall be a little academe,
Still and contemplative in living art.
You three, Berowne, Dumaine, and Longaville,
Have sworn for three years' term to live with me,
My fellow-scholars, and to keep those statutes
That are recorded in this schedule here.
Your oaths are passed; and now subscribe your names,
That his own hand may strike his honour down   20
That violates the smallest branch herein.
If you are armed to do, as sworn to do,
Subscribe to your deep oaths, and keep it too.
Longaville. I am resolved—'tis but a three years' fast:
The mind shall banquet, though the body pine.
Fat paunches have lean pates; and dainty bits

Make rich the ribs, but bankrupt quite the wits.
  Dumaine. My loving lord, Dumaine is mortified.
The grosser manner of these world's delights
30 He throws upon the gross world's baser slaves.
To love, to wealth, to pomp, I pine and die—
With all these living in philosophy.
  Berowne. I can but say their protestation over—
So much, dear liege, I have already sworn,
That is, to live and study here three years.
But there are other strict observances:
As not to see a woman in that term,
Which I hope well is not enrolléd there—
And one day in a week to touch no food,
40 And but one meal on every day beside,
The which I hope is not enrolléd there—
And then to sleep but three hours in the night
And not be seen to wink of all the day,
When I was wont to think no harm all night,
And make a dark night too of half the day,
Which I hope well is not enrolléd there.
O, these are barren tasks, too hard to keep,
Not to see ladies, study, fast, not sleep.
  King. Your oath is passed to pass away from these.
50 *Berowne.* Let me say no, my liege, an if you please.
I only swore to study with your grace,
And stay here in your court for three years' space.
  Longaville. You swore to that, Berowne, and to
    the rest.
  Berowne. By yea and nay, sir, then I swore in jest.
What is the end of study? let me know.
  King. Why, that to know which else we should
    not know.
  Berowne. Things hid and barred, you mean, from
    common sense?

King. Ay, that is study's god-like recompense.

Berowne. Com' on then—I will swear to study so,
To know the thing I am forbid to know: 60
As thus—to study where I well may dine
    When I to feast expressly am forbid,
Or study where to meet some mistress fine
    When mistresses from common sense are hid,
Or, having sworn too hard-a-keeping oath,
Study to break it and not break my troth.
If study's gain be thus, and this be so,
Study knows that which yet it doth not know.
Swear me to this, and I will ne'er say no.

King. These be the stops that hinder study quite,   70
And train our intellects to vain delight.

Berowne. Why, all delights are vain, but that most vain
Which, with pain purchased, doth inherit pain—
As painfully to pore upon a book
    To seek the light of truth, while truth the while
Doth falsely blind the eyesight of his look:
    Light, seeking light, doth light of light beguile:
So, ere you find where light in darkness lies,
Your light grows dark by losing of your eyes.
Study me how to please the eye indeed,   80
    By fixing it upon a fairer eye,
Who dazzling so, that eye shall be his heed,
    And give him light that it was blinded by.
Study is like the heaven's glorious sun,
    That will not be deep-searched with saucy looks:
Small have continual plodders ever won,
    Save base authority from others' books.
These earthly godfathers of heaven's lights
    That give a name to every fixéd star
Have no more profit of their shining nights,   90
    Than those that walk and wot not what they are.

Too much to know is to know nought but fame;
And every godfather can give a name.
  King. How well he's read, to reason against reading.
  Dumaine. Proceeded well, to stop all good proceeding.
  Longaville. He weeds the corn and still lets grow
    the weeding.
  Berowne. The spring is near when green geese
    are a-breeding.
  Dumaine. How follows that?
  Berowne.   Fit in his place and time.
  Dumaine. In reason nothing.
  Berowne.   Something then in rhyme.
100 *King.* Berowne is like an envious sneaping frost
    That bites the first-born infants of the spring.
  Berowne. Well, say I am—why should proud
    summer boast,
  Before the birds have any cause to sing?
Why should I joy in an abortive birth?
At Christmas I no more desire a rose
Than wish a snow in May's new-fangled shows;
But like of each thing that in season grows.
So you to study now it is too late,
Climb o'er the house to unlock the little gate.
110 *King.* Well, sit you out: go home Berowne: adieu!
  Berowne. No my good lord, I have sworn to stay
    with you.
And though I have for barbarism spoke more
  Than for that angel knowledge you can say,
Yet confident I'll keep what I have swore,
  And bide the penance of each three years' day.
Give me the paper, let me read the same,
And to the strictest decrees I'll write my name.
  King. How well this yielding rescues thee
    from shame.

Berowne [*reads*]. 'Item, That no woman shall come
within a mile of my court....' Hath this been pro-   120
claimed?

Longaville. Four days ago.

Berowne. Let's see the penalty. [*reads*] '...on pain of
losing her tongue.' Who devised this penalty?

Longaville. Marry, that did I.

Berowne. Sweet lord, and why?

Longaville. To fright them hence with that
   dread penalty.

Berowne. A dangerous law against gentility....[*reads*]
   'Item, If any man be seen to talk with a woman
within the term of three years, he shall endure such   130
public shame as the rest of the court can possible
devise,'
This article, my liege, yourself must break,
   For well you know here comes in embassy
The French king's daughter with yourself to speak—
   A maid of grace and cómplete majesty—
About surrender up of Aquitaine
   To her decrepit, sick, and bedrid father.
Therefore this article is made in vain,
   Or vainly comes th'admiréd princess hither.   140

King. What say you lords? why, this was quite forgot.

Berowne. So study evermore is overshot.
While it doth study to have what it would,
It doth forget to do the thing it should:
And when it hath the thing it hunteth most,
'Tis won, as towns with fire—so won, so lost.

King. We must of force dispense with this decree.
She must lie here on mere necessity.

Berowne. Necessity will make us all forsworn
   Three thousand times within this three years' space: 150
For every man with his affects is born,

Not by might mast'red, but by special grace.
If I break faith, this word shall speak for me,
I am forsworn 'on mere necessity.'
So to the laws at large I write my name,
    And he that breaks them in the least degree
Stands in attainder of eternal shame.
    Suggestions are to other as to me:
But I believe, although I seem so loath,
160 I am the last that will last keep his oath.... [*he subscribes*
But is there no quick recreation granted?
    King. Ay that there is, our court you know
        is haunted
    With a refinéd traveller of Spain—
A man in all the world's new fashion planted,
    That hath a mint of phrases in his brain:
One who the music of his own vain tongue
    Doth ravish like enchanting harmony:
A man of complements, whom right and wrong
    Have chose as umpire of their mutiny.
170 This child of fancy, that Armado hight,
    For interim to our studies shall relate
In high-born words the worth of many a knight
    From tawny Spain lost in the world's debate.
How you delight, my lords, I know not I,
But I protest I love to hear him lie,
And I will use him for my minstrelsy.
    Berowne. Armado is a most illustrious wight.
A man of fire-new words, fashion's own knight.
    Longaville. Costard the swain and he shall be
        our sport,
180 And so to study three years is but short.

DULL, the constable, and COSTARD, the clown, approach

    Dull. Which is the duke's own person?

Berowne. This, fellow. What wouldst?

Dull. I myself reprehend his own person, for I am his grace's farborough. But I would see his own person in flesh and blood.

Berowne. This is he.

Dull. Signior Arm—Arm—commends you.... [*he presents a letter*] There's villainy abroad. This letter will tell you more.

Costard. Sir, the contempts thereof are as touching me. 190

King. A letter from the magnificent Armado.

Berowne. How low soever the matter, I hope in God for high words.

Longaville. A high hope for a low heaven. God grant us patience.

Berowne. To hear, or forbear hearing?

Longaville. To hear meekly sir, and to laugh moderately—or to forbear both.

Berowne. Well sir, be it as the style shall give us cause to climb in the merriness. 200

Costard. The matter is to me, sir, as concerning Jaquenetta:
The manner of it is, I was taken with the manner.

Berowne. In what manner?

Costard. In manner and form following, sir—all those three: I was seen with her in the manor-house, sitting with her upon the form, and taken following her into the park: which put together, is in manner and form following. Now sir for the manner—it is the manner of a man to speak to a woman. For the form—in some form.

Berowne. For the following, sir? 210

Costard. As it shall follow in my correction—and God defend the right.

King. Will you hear this letter with attention?

Berowne. As we would hear an oracle.

Costard. Such is the simplicity of man to hearken after the flesh.

King [*reads*]. 'Great Deputy, the welkin's Vice-regent, and sole dominator of Navarre, my soul's earth's God, and body's fost'ring patron:'

220 *Costard.* Not a word of Costard yet.

King [*reads*]. 'So it is,'

Costard. It may be so: but if he say it is so, he is, in telling true—but so.

King. Peace!

Costard. —be to me, and every man that dares not fight.

King. No words.

Costard. —of other men's secrets I beseech you.

King [*reads*]. 'So it is, besieged with sable-coloured
230 melancholy, I did commend the black-oppressing humour to the most wholesome physic of thy health-giving air: And, as I am a gentleman, betook myself to walk: the time When? about the sixth hour, When Beasts most graze, Birds best peck, and Men sit down to that nourishment which is called Supper: So much for the time When. Now for the ground Which? which I mean I walked upon, it is ycleped Thy Park. Then for the place Where? where I mean I did encounter that obscene and most prepostrous event, that draweth
240 from my snow-white pen the ebon-coloured Ink, which here thou viewest, beholdest, surveyest, or seest. But to the place Where? It standeth North North-east and by East from the West corner of thy curious-knotted garden. There did I see that low-spirited Swain, that base Minion of thy mirth,'

Costard. Me?

King. 'that unlettered small-knowing soul,'

Costard. Me?

King. 'that shallow vassal,'

Costard. Still me?   250

King. 'which, as I remember, hight Costard,'

Costard. O me!

King. 'sorted and consorted, contrary to thy established proclaimed Edict and continent Canon, †with, with, O with, but with this I passion to say wherewith:'

Costard. With a wench.

King. 'with a child of our Grandmother Eve, a female; or for thy more sweet understanding a Woman: him, I (as my ever-esteemed duty pricks me on) have sent to thee, to receive the meed of punishment, by thy 260 sweet Grace's Officer, Antony Dull, a man of good repute, carriage, bearing, and estimation.'

Dull. Me, an't shall please you! I am Antony Dull.

King. 'For Jaquenetta (so is the weaker vessel called) which I apprehended with the aforesaid Swain, I keep here as a vessel of thy Law's fury, and shall at the least of thy sweet notice, bring her to trial. Thine, in all complements of devoted and heart-burning heat of duty,

DON ADRIANO DE ARMADO.'

Berowne. This is not so well as I looked for, but the 270 best that ever I heard.

King. Ay, the best for the worst.... But sirrah, what say you to this?

Costard. Sir I confess the wench.

King. Did you hear the proclamation?

Costard. I do confess much of the hearing it, but little of the marking of it.

King. It was proclaimed a year's imprisonment to be taken with a wench.

Costard. I was taken with none sir, I was taken with 280 a damsel.

King. Well, it was proclaimed 'damsel.'

Costard. This was no damsel neither sir, she was a virgin.

King. It is so varied too, for it was proclaimed 'virgin.'

Costard. If it were, I deny her virginity: I was taken with a maid.

King. This 'maid' will not serve your turn, sir.

Costard. This maid will serve my turn, sir.

290 *King.* Sir I will pronounce your sentence: you shall fast a week with bran and water.

Costard. I had rather pray a month with mutton and porridge.

King. And Don Armado shall be your keeper.
My Lord Berowne see him delivered o'er—
And go we lords to put in practice that
   Which each to other hath so strongly sworn.
      [*the King, Longaville and Dumaine enter the gates*
Berowne. I'll lay my head to any goodman's hat,
   These oaths and laws will prove an idle scorn—
300 Sirrah, come on.

Costard. I suffer for the truth, sir: for true it is, I was taken with Jaquenetta, and Jaquenetta is a true girl, and therefore welcome the sour cup of prosperity. Affliction may one day smile again, and till then sit thee down, sorrow.   [*they enter the gates*

[1. 2.] *Armado and Moth come through the trees*

Armado. Boy, what sign is it when a man of great spirit grows melancholy?

Moth. A great sign sir that he will look sad.

Armado. Why, sadness is one and the self-same thing, dear imp.

Moth. No no, O Lord sir, no.

Armado. How canst thou part sadness and melancholy, my tender juvenal?

Moth. By a familiar demonstration of the working, my tough signior.   10

Armado. Why tough signior? why tough signior?

Moth. Why tender juvenal? why tender juvenal?

Armado. I spoke it, tender juvenal, as a congruent epitheton appertaining to thy young days, which we may nominate tender.

Moth. And I, tough signior, as an appertinent title to your old time, which we may name tough.

Armado. Pretty and apt.

Moth. How mean you sir, I pretty, and my saying apt? or I apt, and my saying pretty?   20

Armado. Thou pretty, because little.

Moth. Little pretty, because little: wherefore apt?

Armado. And therefore apt, because quick.

Moth. Speak you this in my praise, master?

Armado. In thy condign praise.

Moth. I will praise an eel with the same praise.

Armado. What, that an eel is ingenious?

Moth. That an eel is quick.

Armado. I do say thou art quick in answers. Thou heat'st my blood.   30

Moth. I am answered, sir.

Armado. I love not to be crossed.

(*Moth.* He speaks the mere contrary, crosses love not him.

Armado. I have promised to study three years with the duke.

Moth. You may do it in an hour, sir.

Armado. Impossible.

Moth. How many is one thrice told?

40 *Armado.* I am ill at reck'ning, it fitteth the spirit of a tapster.

Moth. You are a gentleman and a gamester, sir.

Armado. I confess both—they are both the varnish of a complete man.

Moth. Then I am sure you know how much the gross sum of deuce-ace amounts to.

Armado. It doth amount to one more than two.

Moth. Which the base vulgar do call three.

Armado. True.

50 *Moth.* Why sir, is this such a piece of study? Now here is three studied ere ye'll thrice wink: and how easy it is to put 'years' to the word 'three,' and study 'three years' in two words, the dancing horse will tell you.

Armado. A most fine figure!

(*Moth.* To prove you a cipher.

Armado. I will hereupon confess I am in love: and as it is base for a soldier to love, so am I in love with a base wench. If drawing my sword against the humour of affection would deliver me from the reprobate

60 thought of it, I would take Desire prisoner, and ransom him to any French courtier for a new-devised curtsy. I think scorn to sigh—methinks I should outswear Cupid....Comfort me, boy. What great men have been in love?

Moth. Hercules, master.

Armado. Most sweet Hercules! More authority, dear boy, name more; and, sweet my child, let them be men of good repute and carriage.

Moth. Samson, master—he was a man of good carriage,

70 great carriage: for he carried the town-gates on his back like a porter: and he was in love.

Armado. O well-knit Samson! strong-jointed Samson! I do excel thee in my rapier as much as thou didst me in carrying gates. I am in love too. Who was Samson's love, my dear Moth?

Moth. A woman, master.

Armado. Of what complexion?

Moth. Of all the four, or the three, or the two, or one of the four.

Armado. Tell me precisely of what complexion?   80

Moth. Of the sea-water green, sir.

Armado. Is that one of the four complexions?

Moth. As I have read sir, and the best of them too.

Armado. Green indeed is the colour of lovers: but to have a love of that colour, methinks Samson had small reason for it. He surely affected her for her wit.

Moth. It was so sir—for she had a green wit.

Armado. My love is most immaculate white and red.

Moth. Most maculate thoughts, master, are masked under such colours.   90

Armado. Define, define, well-educated infant.

Moth. My father's wit, and my mother's tongue assist me!

Armado. Sweet invocation of a child, most pretty and pathetical.

Moth. If she be made of white and red,
     Her faults will ne'er be known;
   For blushing cheeks by faults are bred,
     And fears by pale white shown:
   Then if she fear, or be to blame,   100
     By this you shall not know,
   For still her cheeks possess the same,
     Which native she doth owe.

A dangerous rhyme, master, against the reason of white and red.

Armado. Is there not a ballad, boy, of the King and the Beggar?

Moth. The world was very guilty of such a ballad some three ages since, but I think now 'tis not to be
110 found: or if it were, it would neither serve for the writing nor the tune.

Armado. I will have that subject newly writ o'er, that I may example my digression by some mighty precedent. Boy, I do love—that country girl that I took in the park with the rational hind Costard: she deserves well.

(*Moth.* To be whipped: and yet a better love than my master.

Armado. Sing, boy. My spirit grows heavy in love.

(*Moth.* And that's great marvel, loving a light wench.
120 *Armado.* I say, sing.

Moth. Forbear till this company be past.

DULL, COSTARD, *and* JAQUENETTA *come forth*

Dull. Sir, the duke's pleasure is that you keep Costard safe—and you must suffer him to take no delight, nor no penance, but a' must fast three days a week. For this damsel, I must keep her at the park—she is allowed for the dey-woman. Fare you well.   [*he turns away*

Armado. I do betray myself with blushing. Maid!

Jaquenetta. Man.

Armado. I will visit thee at the lodge.
130 *Jaquenetta.* That's hereby.

Armado. I know where it is situate.

Jaquenetta. Lord, how wise you are!

Armado. I will tell thee wonders.

Jaquenetta. With that face?

Armado. I love thee.

Jaquenetta. So I heard you say.

Armado. And so farewell.

Jaquenetta. Fair weather after you!

Dull [*calls*]. Come Jaquenetta, away.

[*Dull and Jaquenetta re-enter the gates*

Armado. Villain, thou shalt fast for thy offences ere 140
thou be pardoned.

Costard. Well sir, I hope when I do it, I shall do it
on a full stomach.

Armado. Thou shalt be heavily punished.

Costard. I am more bound to you than your fellows,
for they are but lightly rewarded.

Armado. Take away this villain, shut him up.

Moth. Come you transgressing slave, away.

Costard. Let me not be pent up sir, I will fast being loose.

Moth. No sir, that were fast and loose: thou shalt to 150
prison.

Costard. Well, if ever I do see the merry days of
desolation that I have seen, some shall see—

Moth. What shall some see?

Costard. Nay nothing, Master Moth, but what they
look upon. It is not for prisoners to be too silent in
their words, and therefore I will say nothing: I thank
God I have as little patience as another man, and therefore I can be quiet. [*Moth and Costard depart*

Armado. I do affect the very ground (which is base) 160
where her shoe (which is baser) guided by her foot
(which is basest) doth tread. I shall be forsworn
(which is a great argument of falsehood) if I love.
And how can that be true love, which is falsely at-
tempted? Love is a familiar; love is a devil. There is
no evil angel but love. Yet was Samson so tempted, and
he had an excellent strength: yet was Solomon so
seduced, and he had a very good wit. Cupid's butt-shaft
is too hard for Hercules' club, and therefore too much
odds for a Spaniard's rapier. The first and second cause 170
will not serve my turn: the passado he respects not, the

duello he regards not; his disgrace is to be called boy,
but his glory is to subdue men. Adieu valour, rust
rapier, be still drum! for your manager is in love; yea
he loveth. Assist me some extemporal god of rhyme,
for I am sure I shall turn sonnet. Devise wit, write pen,
for I am for whole volumes in folio.   [*he goes*

[2. 1.] *The* PRINCESS OF FRANCE, ROSALINE (*a black-
eyed, black-haired beauty*), MARIA, KATHARINE, BOYET,
lords and other attendants draw near the gates

  Boyet. Now, madam, summon up your
    dearest spirits,
Consider who the king your father sends.
To whom he sends, and what's his embassy.
Yourself, held precious in the world's esteem,
To parley with the sole inheritor
Of all perfections that a man may owe,
Matchless Navarre; the plea of no less weight
Than Aquitaine, a dowry for a queen.
Be now as prodigal of all dear grace,
10 As nature was in making graces dear,
When she did starve the general world beside,
And prodigally gave them all to you.
  Princess. Good Lord Boyet, my beauty, though
    but mean,
Needs not the painted flourish of your praise:
Beauty is bought by judgement of the eye,
Not utt'red by base sale of chapmen's tongues.
I am less proud to hear you tell my worth
Than you much willing to be counted wise
In spending your wit in the praise of mine.

But now to task the tasker—good Boyet,　　　　20
You are not ignorant all-telling fame
Doth noise abroad Navarre hath made a vow,
Till painful study shall outwear three years,
No woman may approach his silent court:
Therefore to's seemeth it a needful course,
Before we enter his forbidden gates,
To know his pleasure; and in that behalf,
Bold of your worthiness, we single you,
As our best-moving fair solicitor.
Tell him, the daughter of the King of France,　　30
On serious business craving quick dispatch,
Importunes personal conference with his grace.
Haste, signify so much, while we attend,
Like humble-visaged suitors, his high will.
　Boyet. Proud of employment, willingly I go.
　Princess. All pride is willing pride, and yours is so.
　　　　　　　　　　　　[he enters the gates
Who are the votaries, my loving lords,
That are vow-fellows with this virtuous duke?
　A lord. Lord Longaville is one.
　Princess.　　　　　　　Know you the man?
　Maria. I know him, madam: at a marriage-feast,　40
Between Lord Perigort and the beauteous heir
Of Jaquës Falconbridge, solemnizéd
In Normandy, saw I this Longaville.
A man of sovereign parts he is esteemed;
Well fitted in arts, glorious in arms:
Nothing becomes him ill that he would well.
The only soil of his fair virtue's gloss—
If virtue's gloss will stain with any soil—
Is a sharp wit matched with too blunt a will;
Whose edge hath power to cut, whose will still wills　50
It should none spare that come within his power.

Princess. Some merry mocking lord belike, is't so?
Maria. They say so most that most his humours know.
Princess. Such short-lived wits do wither as they grow.
Who are the rest?
 Katharine. The young Dumaine, a well-accom-
  plished youth,
Of all that virtue love for virtue loved:
Most power to do most harm, least knowing ill;
For he hath wit to make an ill shape good,
60 And shape to win grace though he had no wit.
I saw him at the Duke Alanson's once,
And much too little of that good I saw
Is my report to his great worthiness.
 Rosaline. Another of these students at that time
Was there with him, if I have heard a truth—
Berowne they call him—but a merrier man,
Within the limit of becoming mirth,
I never spent an hour's talk withal.
His eye begets occasion for his wit,
70 For every object that the one doth catch
The other turns to a mirth-moving jest,
Which his fair tongue—conceit's expositor—
Delivers in such apt and gracious words,
That agèd ears play truant at his tales,
And younger hearings are quite ravishèd,
So sweet and voluble is his discourse.
 Princess. God bless my ladies! are they all in love,
That every one her own hath garnishèd
With such bedecking ornaments of praise?

    BOYET returns

80 *A lord.* Here comes Boyet.
 Princess.   Now, what admittance, lord?
 Boyet. Navarre had notice of your fair approach,

And he and his competitors in oath
Were all addressed to meet you, gentle lady,
Before I came. Marry, thus much I have learnt:
He rather means to lodge you in the field,
Like one that comes here to besiege his court,
Than seek a dispensation for his oath,
To let you enter his unpeopled house.
Here comes Navarre.

The KING, LONGAVILLE, DUMAINE, BEROWNE
and attendants come forth. [*The ladies mask*]

King. Fair princess, welcome to the court of Navarre. 90
Princess. 'Fair' I give you back again, and 'welcome'
I have not yet: the roof of this court is too high to be
yours, and welcome to the wide fields too base to be mine.
King. You shall be welcome, madam, to my court.
Princess. I will be welcome then—conduct me thither.
King. Hear me dear lady, I have sworn an oath.
Princess. Our Lady help my lord! he'll be forsworn.
King. Not for the world fair madam, by my will.
Princess. Why, will shall break it; will, and
      nothing else.
King. Your ladyship is ignorant what it is.   100
Princess. Were my lord so, his ignorance were wise,
Where now his knowledge must prove ignorance.
I hear your grace hath sworn out house-keeping:
'Tis deadly sin to keep that oath, my lord,
And sin to break it.
But pardon me, I am too sudden-bold—
To teach a teacher ill beseemeth me.
Vouchsafe to read the purpose of my coming,
And suddenly resolve me in my suit. [*she gives a paper*
  King. Madam I will, if suddenly I may.   110

Princess. You will the sooner that I were away,
For you'll prove perjured if you make me stay.

                  [the King peruses the paper

[Berowne. Did not I dance with you in Brabant once?]
Katharine. Did not I dance with you in Brabant once?
Berowne. I know you did.
Katharine.   How needless was it then
To ask the question!
Berowne.   You must not be so quick.
Katharine. 'Tis 'long of you that spur me with
    such questions.
Berowne. Your wit's too hot, it speeds too fast,
    'twill tire.
Katharine. Not till it leave the rider in the mire.
120 *Berowne.* What time o' day?
Katharine.   The hour that fools should ask.
Berowne. Now fair befall your mask!
Katharine. Fair fall the face it covers!
Berowne. And send you many lovers!
Katharine. Amen, so you be none.
[*Berowne.* Nay then will I be gone.   ]
  King. Madam, your father here doth intimate
The payment of a hundred thousand crowns,
Being but the one half of an entire sum
Disbursèd by my father in his wars.
130 But say that he, or we—as neither have—
Received that sum, yet there remains unpaid
A hundred thousand more, in surety of the which
One part of Aquitaine is bound to us,
Although not valued to the money's worth.
If then the king your father will restore
But that one half which is unsatisfied,
We will give up our right in Aquitaine,
And hold fair friendship with his majesty.

But that, it seems, he little purposeth,
For here he doth demand to have repaid   140
A hundred thousand crowns, and not demands,
On payment of a hundred thousand crowns,
To have his title live in Aquitaine;
Which we much rather had depart withal,
And have the money by our father lent,
Than Aquitaine, so gelded as it is.
Dear princess, were not his requests so far
From reason's yielding, your fair self should make
A yielding 'gainst some reason in my breast,
And go well satisfied to France again.   150
    Princess. You do the king my father too much wrong,
And wrong the reputation of your name,
In so unseeming to confess receipt
Of that which hath so faithfully been paid.
    King. I do protest I never heard of it:
And if you prove it, I'll repay it back
Or yield up Aquitaine.
    Princess.   We arrest your word.
Boyet, you can produce acquittances
For such a sum from special officers
Of Charles his father.
    King.   Satisfy me so.   160
    Boyet. So please your grace, the packet is not come
Where that and other specialties are bound:
To-morrow you shall have a sight of them.
    King. It shall suffice me; at which interview
All liberal reason I will yield unto.
Meantime, receive such welcome at my hand
As honour—without breach of honour—may
Make tender of to thy true worthiness.
You may not come, fair princess, within my gates,
But here without you shall be so received,   170

As you shall deem yourself lodged in my heart,
Though so denied fair harbour in my house.
Your own good thoughts excuse me, and farewell—
To-morrow shall we visit you again.
   Princess. Sweet health and fair desires consort
     your grace!
   King. Thy own wish wish I thee in every place!
               [*the King and his train re-enter the gates*
[*Berowne.* Lady, I will commend you to mine own]
heart.
   Rosaline. Pray you, do my commendations—I would
180 be glad to see it.
   Berowne. I would you heard it groan.
   Rosaline. Is the fool sick?
   Berowne. Sick at the heart.
   Rosaline. Alack, let it blood.
   Berowne. Would that do it good?
   Rosaline. My physic says, 'ay.'
   Berowne. Will you prick't with your eye?
   Rosaline. No point, with my knife.
   Berowne. Now God save thy life!
190   *Rosaline.* And yours from long living!
[*Berowne.* I cannot stay thanksgiving.   ]

DUMAINE *returns*

   Dumaine. Sir, I pray you a word. What lady is
     that same?
   Boyet. †The heir of Alanson, Katharine her name.
   Dumaine. A gallant lady. Monsieur, fare you well.
                        [*he goes*

LONGAVILLE *returns*

   Longaville. I beseech you a word. What is she in
     the white?
   Boyet. A woman sometimes, an you saw her in the light.

Longaville. Perchance light in the light. I desire
her name.

Boyet. She hath but one for herself—to desire that
were a shame.

Longaville. Pray you sir, whose daughter?

Boyet. Her mother's, I have heard.   200

Longaville. God's blessing on your beard!

Boyet. Good sir be not offended.
She is an heir of Falconbridge.

Longaville. Nay, my choler is ended.
She is a most sweet lady.

Boyet. Not unlike, sir, that may be. [*Longaville goes*

BEROWNE *returns*

Berowne. What's her name in the cap?

Boyet. †Rosaline by good hap.

Berowne. Is she wedded or no?

Boyet. To her will sir, or so.   210

Berowne. You are welcome sir, adieu.

Boyet. Farewell to me sir, and welcome to you.
[*Berowne goes*

Maria. That last is Berowne, the merry mad-cap lord—
Not a word with him but a jest.

Boyet.   And every jest but a word.

Princess. It was well done of you to take him at
his word.

Boyet. I was as willing to grapple as he was to board.

Katharine. Two hot sheeps, marry!

Boyet.   And wherefore not ships?
No sheep, sweet lamb, unless we feed on your lips.

Katharine. You sheep, and I pasture: shall that finish
the jest?

Boyet. So you grant pasture for me.   220
[*he offers to kiss her*

Katharine.   Not so, gentle beast—
My lips are no common, though several they be.
   Boyet. Belonging to whom?
   Katharine.   To my fortunes and me.
   Princess. Good wits will be jangling, but gentles agree.
This civil war of wits were much better used
On Navarre and his book-men, for here 'tis abused.
   Boyet. If my observation—which very seldom lies—
By the heart's still rhetoric discloséd with eyes,
Deceive me not now, Navarre is infected.
   Princess. With what?
230 *Boyet.* With that which we lovers entitle 'affected.'
   Princess. Your reason?
   Boyet. Why, all his behaviours did make their retire
To the court of his eye, peeping thorough desire.
His heart like an agate with your print impressed,
Proud with his form, in his eye pride expresséd.
His tongue all impatient to speak and not see,
Did stumble with haste in his eyesight to be.
All senses to that sense did make their repair,
To feel only looking on fairest of fair:
240 Methought all his senses were locked in his eye,
As jewels in crystal for some prince to buy,
Who, tend'ring their own worth from where they
     were glassed,
Did point you to buy them, along as you passed.
His face's own margent did quote such amazes,
That all eyes saw his eyes enchanted with gazes.
I'll give you Aquitaine, and all that is his,
An you give him for my sake but one loving kiss.
   Princess. Come, to our pavilion! Boyet is disposed.
   Boyet. But to speak that in words which his eye
     hath disclosed.
250 I only have made a mouth of his eye,

By adding a tongue which I know will not lie.

Rosaline. Thou art an old love-monger, and
 speakest skilfully.

Maria. He is Cupid's grandfather, and learns news
 of him.

Katharine. Then was Venus like her mother, for her
 father is but grim.

Boyet. Do you hear, my mad wenches?

Maria.   No.

Boyet.   What then, do you see?

Rosaline. †Ay, our way to be gone.

Boyet.   You are too hard for me.
            [they go

     A day passes

[3. 1.] *ARMADO and MOTH seated beneath the trees*

Armado. Warble, child, make passionate my sense
of hearing.

Moth [singing]. Concolinel.

Armado. Sweet air! Go, tenderness of years, take this
key, give enlargement to the swain, bring him festinately hither. I must employ him in a letter to
my love.

Moth. Master, will you win your love with a French
brawl?

Armado. How meanest thou? brawling in French? 10

Moth. No, my complete master—but to jig off a tune
at the tongue's end, canary to it with your feet, humour
it with turning up your eyelids, sigh a note and sing a
note, sometime through the throat as if you swallowed
love with singing love, sometime through the nose as if
you snuffed up love by smelling love, with your hat
penthouse-like o'er the shop of your eyes, with your
arms crossed on your thin-belly doublet like a rabbit on

a spit, or your hands in your pocket like a man after the
20 old painting—and keep not too long in one tune, but a
snip and away. These are complements, these are
humours, these betray nice wenches that would be
betrayed without these, and make them men of note—
do you note me?—that most are affected to these.

Armado. How hast thou purchased this experience?

Moth. By my penny of observation.

Armado. But O—but O—

Moth. —'the hobby-horse is forgot.'

Armado. Call'st thou my love 'hobby-horse'?

30 *Moth.* No master, the hobby-horse is but a colt—
[*aside*] and your love, perhaps, a hackney....
But have you forgot your love?

Armado. Almost I had.

Moth. Negligent student! learn her by heart.

Armado. By heart, and in heart, boy.

Moth. And out of heart, master: all those three I will
prove.

Armado. What wilt thou prove?

Moth. A man, if I live—and this 'by, in, and without,'
40 upon the instant. By heart you love her, because your
heart cannot come by her: in heart you love her,
because your heart is in love with her: and out of heart
you love her, being out of heart that you cannot enjoy
her.

Armado. I am all these three.

Moth. And three times as much more—[*aside*] and yet
nothing at all.

Armado. Fetch hither the swain. He must carry me
a letter.

50 *Moth.* A message well sympathized—a horse to be
ambassador for an ass!

Armado. Ha? ha? what sayest thou?

Moth. Marry sir, you must send the ass upon the
horse, for he is very slow-gaited. But I go.
Armado. The way is but short—away.
Moth. As swift as lead, sir.
Armado. The meaning, pretty ingenious?
Is not lead a metal heavy, dull, and slow?
Moth. Minime, honest master, or rather master, no.
Armado. I say lead is slow.
Moth. You are too swift, sir, to say so. 60
Is that lead slow which is fired from a gun?
Armado. Sweet smoke of rhetoric!
He reputes me a cannon—and the bullet, that's he:
I shoot thee at the swain.
Moth. Thump then, and I flee. [*he trips away*
Armado. A most acute juvenal, volable and free
of grace!
By thy favour, sweet welkin, I must sigh in thy face:
Most rude melancholy, valour gives thee place.
[*he muses*
My herald is returned.

Moth *returns with* Costard

Moth. A wonder, master! here's a costard broken in
a shin.
Armado. Some enigma, some riddle—come, thy
l'envoy—begin. 70
Costard. No egma, no riddle, no l'envoy, no salve in
the mail, sir. O sir, plantain, a plain plantain! no
l'envoy, no l'envoy, no salve sir, but a plantain!
Armado. By virtue, thou enforcest laughter—thy silly
thought, my spleen. The heaving of my lungs provokes
me to ridiculous smiling: O, pardon me my stars! Doth
the inconsiderate take 'salve' for 'l'envoy,' and the
word l'envoy for a salve?

Moth. Do the wise think them other? is not l'envoy a
80 salve?

Armado. No page, it is an epilogue or discourse to
make plain
Some obscure precedence that hath tofore been sain.
I will example it:

> The Fox, the Ape, and the Humble-bee,
> Were still at odds, being but three.

There's the moral: now the l'envoy.

Moth. I will add the l'envoy. Say the moral again.

Armado. The Fox, the Ape, and the Humble-bee,
Were still at odds, being but three.

90 *Moth.*   Until the Goose came out of door,
And stayed the odds by adding four.

Now will I begin your moral, and do you follow with
my l'envoy.

> The Fox, the Ape, and the Humble-bee,
> Were still at odds, being but three.

Armado. Until the Goose came out of door,
Staying the odds by adding four.

Moth. A good l'envoy, ending in the goose: would
you desire more?

100 *Costard.* The boy hath sold him a bargain, a goose,
that's flat.
Sir, your pennyworth is good, an your goose be fat.
To sell a bargain well is as cunning as fast and loose:
Let me see, a fat l'envoy—ay, that's a fat goose.

Armado. Come hither, come hither. How did this
argument begin?

Moth. By saying that a costard was broken in
a shin—
Then called you for the l'envoy.

Costard. True, and I for a plantain—thus came your
argument in—

Then the boy's fat l'envoy, the goose that you bought—
And he ended the market

Armado. But tell me. How was there a costard broken 110
in a shin?

Moth. I will tell you sensibly.

Costard. Thou hast no feeling of it, Moth—I will
speak that l'envoy.

    I, Costard, running out, that was safely within,
    Fell over the threshold and broke my shin.

Armado. We will talk no more of this matter.

Costard. Till there be more matter in the shin.

Armado. Sirrah Costard, I will enfranchise thee.

Costard. O, marry me to one Frances! I smell some 120
l'envoy, some goose, in this.

Armado. By my sweet soul, I mean setting thee at
liberty, enfreedoming thy person: thou wert immured,
restrained, captivated, bound.

Costard. True, true—and now you will be my purgation, and let me loose.

Armado. I give thee thy liberty, set thee from durance,
and in lieu thereof impose on thee nothing but this!
[*he proffers a letter*] Bear this significant to the country
maid Jaquenetta...[*he bestows a coin upon him*] There 130
is remuneration—for the best ward of mine honour is
rewarding my dependents. Moth, follow. [*he departs*

Moth. Like the sequel, I. Signior Costard, adieu.

              [*he follows Armado, aping his gait*

Costard. My sweet ounce of man's flesh! my
    incony Jew!

Now will I look to his remuneration. [*he opens his palm*]
Remuneration! O, that's the Latin word for three-
farthings: three-farthings—remuneration. 'What's the
price of this inkle?' 'One penny.' 'No, I'll give you
a remuneration': why, it carries it. Remuneration!

140 why, it is a fairer name than French crown. I will
never buy and sell out of this word.

BEROWNE approaches

Berowne. My good knave Costard, exceedingly well met.
Costard. Pray you sir, how much carnation ribbon
may a man buy for a remuneration?
Berowne. What is a remuneration?
Costard. Marry sir, halfpenny farthing.
Berowne. Why then, three-farthing worth of silk.
Costard. I thank your worship. God be wi' you.
                                    [*he turns to go*
Berowne. Stay slave, I must employ thee.
150 As thou wilt win my favour, good my knave,
Do one thing for me that I shall entreat.
Costard. When would you have it done, sir?
Berowne. This afternoon.
Costard. Well, I will do it, sir: fare you well.
Berowne. Thou knowest not what it is.
Costard. I shall know, sir, when I have done it.
Berowne. Why, villain, thou must know first.
Costard. I will come to your worship to-morrow
morning.
160 *Berowne.* It must be done this afternoon. Hark, slave,
it is but this:
The princess comes to hunt here in the park,
And in her train there is a gentle lady:
When tongues spake sweetly, then they name her
    name,
And Rosaline they call her. Ask for her;
And to her white hand see thou do commend
This sealed-up counsel.   [*he gives him a letter and a*
                        shilling] There's thy guerdon: go

Costard. Gardon, O sweet gardon! better than remuneration, eleven-pence farthing better: most sweet
gardon. I will do it, sir, in print! Gardon—remunera- 170
tion!   [*he enters the gates*

Berowne. And I—
Forsooth in love, I that have been love's whip!
A very beadle to a humorous sigh,
A critic, nay, a night-watch constable,
A domineering pedant o'er the boy,
Than whom no mortal so magnificent—
This wimpled, whining, purblind, wayward boy,
This Signior Junior, giant-dwarf, Dan Cupid,
Regent of love-rhymes, lord of folded arms,   180
Th'anointed sovereign of sighs and groans,
Liege of all loiterers and malcontents,
Dread Prince of Plackets, King of Codpieces,
Sole imperator and great general
Of trotting paritors—O my little heart!
And I to be a corporal of his field,
And wear his colours like a tumbler's hoop!
What I! I love! I sue! I seek a wife!
A woman, that is like a German clock,
Still a-repairing, ever out frame,   190
And never going aright, being a watch,
But being watched that it may still go right.
Nay, to be perjured, which is worst of all;
And among three to love the worst of all—
A whitely wanton with a velvet brow,
With two pitch-balls stuck in her face for eyes,
Ay and, by heaven, one that will do the deed,
Though Argus were her eunuch and her guard!
And I to sigh for her, to watch for her,
To pray for her, go to: it is a plague   200
That Cupid will impose for my neglect

Of his almighty dreadful little might.
Well, I will love, write, sigh, pray, sue, and groan—
Some men must love my lady, and some Joan.   [*he goes*

[4. 1.] *The* PRINCESS, ROSALINE, MARIA, KATHA-
RINE, BOYET, *lords, attendants, and a Forester draw near*

Princess. Was that the king that spurred his horse
    so hard
Against the steep-up rising of the hill?
    Boyet. I know not, but I think it was not he.
    Princess. Whoe'er a' was, a' showed a mounting mind.
Well lords, to-day we shall have our dispatch,
On Saturday we will return to France.
Then, forester, my friend, where is the bush
That we must stand and play the murderer in?
    Forester. Hereby upon the edge of yonder coppice—
10 A stand where you may make the fairest shoot.
    Princess. I thank my beauty, I am fair that shoot,
And thereupon thou speak'st the fairest shoot.
    Forester. Pardon me madam, for I meant not so.
    Princess. What, what! first praise me, and again say no?
O short-lived pride. Not fair? alack for woe!
    Forester. Yes madam, fair.
    Princess.   Nay, never paint me now.
Where fair is not, praise cannot mend the brow.
Here—good my glass!—take this for telling true:
                        [*she gives him money*
Fair payment for foul words is more than due.
20 *Forester.* Nothing but fair is that which you inherit.
    Princess. See, see, my beauty will be saved by merit!
O heresy in fair, fit for these days!
A giving hand, though foul, shall have fair praise.

But come, the bow: now mercy goes to kill,
And shooting well is then accounted ill.
Thus will I save my credit in the shoot:
Not wounding, pity would not let me do't;
If wounding, then it was to show my skill,
That more for praise than purpose meant to kill.
And, out of question, so it is sometimes: 30
Glory grows guilty of detested crimes,
When, for fame's sake, for praise, an outward part,
We bend to that the working of the heart:
As I for praise alone now seek to spill
The poor deer's blood, that my heart means no ill.

Boyet. Do not curst wives hold that self sovereignty
Only for praise sake, when they strive to be
Lords o'er their lords?

Princess. Only for praise—and praise we may afford
To any lady that subdues a lord.   40

COSTARD *comes forth*

Princess. Here comes a member of the commonwealth.

Costard. God dig-you-den all, pray you which is the
head lady?

Princess. Thou shalt know her, fellow, by the rest
that have no heads.

Costard. Which is the greatest lady, the highest?

Princess. The thickest, and the tallest.

Costard. The thickest and the tallest! It is so—truth
   is truth.
An your waist, mistress, were as slender as my wit,
One o' these maids' girdles for your waist should be fit. 50
Are not you the chief woman? you are the thickest here.

Princess. What's your will, sir? what's your will?

Costard. I have a letter from Monsieur Berowne, to
   one Lady Rosaline.

Princess. O, thy letter, thy letter: he's a good friend
      of mine.   [*she snatches the letter*
Stand aside, good bearer. Boyet, you can carve.
Break up this capon.
      Boyet [*bows*].   I am bound to serve.
                          [*he glances at the superscription*
This letter is mistook: it importeth none here.
It is writ to Jaquenetta.
      Princess.   We will read it, I swear.
Break the neck of the wax, and every one give ear.

'*Boyet reads*'

60 'By heaven, that thou art fair is most infallible; true
that thou art beauteous; truth itself that thou art lovely.
More fairer than fair, beautiful than beauteous, truer
than truth itself, have commiseration on thy heroical
vassal. The magnanimous and most illustrate King
Cophetua set eye upon the penurious and indubitate
beggar Zenelophon: and he it was that might rightly say
'veni, vidi, vici': which to anatomize in the vulgar—
O base and obscure vulgar!—videlicet, he came, saw, and
overcame: he came, one; saw, two; overcame, three.
70 Who came? the king. Why did he come? to see. Why
did he see? to overcome. To whom came he? to the
beggar. What saw he? the beggar. Who overcame he?
the beggar. The conclusion is victory: on whose
side? the king's: the captive is enriched—on whose side?
the beggar's. The catastrophe is a nuptial—on whose
side? the king's: no, on both in one, or one in both.
I am the king, for so stands the comparison—thou the
beggar, for so witnesseth thy lowliness. Shall I command thy love? I may. Shall I enforce thy love? I
80 could. Shall I entreat thy love? I will. What shalt thou
exchange for rags?—robes. For tittles?—titles. For thy-

self?—me! Thus expecting thy reply, I profane my lips
on thy foot, my eyes on thy picture, and my heart on
thy every part.

    Thine in the dearest design of industry,
      Don Adriano de Armado.
 Thus dost thou hear the Nemean lion roar
  'Gainst thee, thou lamb, that standest as his prey:
 Submissive fall his princely feet before,
  And he from forage will incline to play.   90
 But if thou strive, poor soul, what art thou then?
 Food for his rage, repasture for his den.'
Princess. What plume of feathers is he that indited
 this letter?
What vane? what weathercock? did you ever
 hear better?
Boyet. I am much deceived but I remember
 the style.
Princess. Else your memory is bad, going o'er
 it erewhile.
Boyet. This Armado is a Spaniard that keeps here
 in court,
A phantasime, a Monarcho, and one that makes sport
To the prince and his book-mates.
 (*Princess* [*beckons him aside*]. Thou, fellow, a word.
Who gave thee this letter?
 (*Costard.*   I told you—my lord.   100
 (*Princess.* To whom shouldst thou give it?
 (*Costard.*   From my lord to my lady.
 (*Princess.* From which lord, to which lady?
 (*Costard.* From my Lord Berowne, a good master
 of mine,
To a lady of France, that he called Rosaline.
 (*Princess.* Thou hast mistaken his letter.   [*turns*]
 Come lords, away.   [*to Rosaline*

Here, sweet, put up this—'twill be thine another day.
[*all depart save Boyet, Rosaline, Maria and Costard*
Boyet. Who is the suitor? who is the suitor?
Rosaline.   Shall I teach you to know?
Boyet. Ay, my continent of beauty.
Rosaline.   Why, she that bears the bow.
Finely put off!
110 *Boyet.* My lady goes to kill horns—but if thou marry,
Hang me by the neck, if horns that year miscarry.
Finely put on!
Rosaline. Well then, I am the shooter.
Boyet.   And who is your deer?
Rosaline. If we choose by the horns, yourself come
    not near.
Finely put on, indeed!
Maria. You still wrangle with her, Boyet, and she
    strikes at the brow.
Boyet. But she herself is hit lower: have I hit
    her now?
Rosaline. Shall I come upon thee with an old saying,
that was a man when King Pepin of France was a little
120 boy, as touching the hit it?
Boyet. So I may answer thee with one as old, that was
a woman when Queen Guinever of Britain was a little
wench, as touching the hit it.

Rosaline and Boyet dance together and sing

Rosaline. Thou canst not hit it, hit it, hit it:
            Thou canst not hit it, my good man.
    Boyet. An I cannot, cannot, cannot:
            An I cannot, another can.
                              [*Rosaline runs away*
Costard [*to Maria*]. By my troth, most pleasant! how
    both did fit it!

Maria. A mark marvellous well shot, for they both
    did hit it.
Boyet [*turns*]. A mark! O mark but that mark: 'A
    mark,' says my lady! 130
Let the mark have a prick in't, to mete at if it may be.
Maria. Wide o' the bow hand! I'faith, your hand
    is out.
Costard. Indeed a' must shoot nearer, or he'll ne'er
    hit the clout.
Boyet. An if my hand be out, then belike your hand
    is in.
Costard. Then will she get the upshoot by cleaving
    the pin.
Maria. Come come, you talk greasily, your lips
    grow foul.
Costard. She's too hard for you at pricks, sir—chal-
    lenge her to bowl.
Boyet. I fear too much rubbing. [*bows*] Good night,
    my good owl. [*Boyet and Maria go off*
Costard. By my soul, a swain, a most simple clown!
Lord, lord, how the ladies and I have put him down! 140
O' my troth, most sweet jests, most incony vulgar wit,
When it comes so smoothly off, so obscenely as it were,
    so fit.
Armado to th'one side, O, a most dainty man.
To see him walk before a lady, and to bear her fan.
To see him kiss his hand, and how most sweetly a'
    will swear!
And his page o' t'other side, that handful of wit!
Ah, heavens, it is a most pathetical nit!

           A shout is heard

Sola, sola! [*he runs off into the coppice*

[4. 2.] *HOLOFERNES, SIR NATHANIEL, and DULL
come up, holding lively conversation*

Sir Nathaniel. Very reverend sport truly, and done in
the testimony of a good conscience.

Holofernes. The deer was, as you know, in sanguis,
blood—ripe as the pomewater who now hangeth like a
jewel in the ear of caelum, the sky, the welkin, the heaven, and anon falleth like a crab on the face of terra, the
soil, the land, the earth.

Sir Nathaniel. Truly, Master Holofernes, the epithets
are sweetly varied, like a scholar at the least: but sir,
10 I assure ye it was a buck of the first head.

Holofernes. Sir Nathaniel, haud credo.

Dull. 'Twas not a haud credo, 'twas a pricket.

Holofernes. Most barbarous intimation! yet a kind of
insinuation, as it were in via, in way, of explication;
facere as it were replication, or rather ostentare, to show
as it were his inclination—after his undressed, un-
polished, uneducated, unpruned, untrained, or rather
unlettered, or ratherest, unconfirmed fashion—to insert
again my haud credo for a deer.

20 *Dull.* I said the deer was not a haud credo, 'twas a
pricket.

Holofernes. Twice sod simplicity, bis coctus!

O thou monster Ignorance, how deformed dost thou look!

Sir Nathaniel. Sir, he hath never fed of the dainties
that are bred in a book.

He hath not eat paper, as it were; he hath not
drunk ink:

His intellect is not replenished, he is only an animal,
only sensible in the duller parts:

And such barren plants are set before us, that we
thankful should be,

Which we of taste and feeling are, for those parts that
　　do fructify in us more than he.
For as it would ill become me to be vain, indiscreet, or
　　a fool,　　　　　　　　　　　　　　　　　　　　　　30
So were there a patch set on learning, to see him in
　　a school:
But omne bene say I, being of an old father's mind,
Many can brook the weather that love not the wind.
　　Dull. You two are book-men—can you tell me by
　　　your wit,
What was a month old at Cain's birth, that's not five
　　weeks old as yet?
　　Holofernes. Dictynna, goodman Dull—Dictynna,
goodman Dull.
　　Dull. What is Dictynna?
　　Sir Nathaniel. A title to Phœbe, to Luna, to the moon.
　　Holofernes. The moon was a month old when Adam
　　　was no more,　　　　　　　　　　　　　　　　　　40
And raught not to five weeks when he came to five-score.
Th'allusion holds in the exchange.
　　Dull. 'Tis true indeed—the collusion holds in the
exchange.
　　Holofernes. God comfort thy capacity! I say, th'allu-
sion holds in the exchange.
　　Dull. And I say, the pollution holds in the exchange;
for the moon is never but a month old. And I say
beside that 'twas a pricket that the princess killed.
　　Holofernes. Sir Nathaniel, will you hear an extemporal 50
epitaph on the death of the deer? and, to humour the
ignorant, I call the deer the princess killed, a pricket.
　　Sir Nathaniel. Perge, good Master Holofernes, perge,
so it shall please you to abrogate scurrility.
　　Holofernes. I will something affect the letter, for it
argues facility.

The preyful princess pierced and pricked
A pretty pleasing pricket—
Some say a sore, but not a sore,
Till now made sore with shooting.
60   The dogs did yell—put 'ell to sore,
Then sorel jumps from thicket;
†Or pricket sore—or else sore'll
The people fall a-hooting.
If sore be sore, then L to sore
Make fifty sores o'sorel:
Of one sore I an hundred make,
By adding but one more L.

Sir Nathaniel. A rare talent!

(*Dull.* If a talent be a claw, look how he claws him
70 with a talent.

Holofernes. This is a gift that I have, simple, simple;
a foolish extravagant spirit, full of forms, figures, shapes,
objects, ideas, apprehensions, motions, revolutions.
These are begot in the ventricle of memory, nourished
in the womb of pia mater, and delivered upon the
mellowing of occasion. But the gift is good in those in
whom it is acute, and I am thankful for it.

Sir Nathaniel. Sir, I praise the Lord for you, and so
may my parishioners, for their sons are well tutored by
80 you, and their daughters profit very greatly under you:
you are a good member of the commonwealth.

Holofernes. Mehercle! if their sons be ingenious, they
shall want no instruction: if their daughters be capable,
I will put it to them. But, vir sapit qui pauca loquitur
—a soul feminine saluteth us.

JAQUENETTA and COSTARD come forth

Jaquenetta. God give you good morrow, Master.
Person

Holofernes. Master Person—quasi pierce-one? And if one should be pierced, which is the one?

Costard. Marry, master schoolmaster, he that is like- 90 liest to a hogshead.

Holofernes. Piercing a hogshead! a good lustre of conceit in a turf of earth, fire enough for a flint, pearl enough for a swine: 'tis pretty, it is well.

Jaquenetta [*delivering a letter*]. Good Master Person, be so good as read me this letter. It was given me by Costard, and sent me from Don Armado: I beseech you, read it. [*Nathaniel peruses the letter*

Holofernes.

'Fauste precor gelida quando pecus omne sub umbra
Ruminat,' and so forth. Ah, good old Mantuan! 100
I may speak of thee as the traveller doth of Venice:
Venetia, Venetia,
Chi non ti vede, non ti pretia.
Old Mantuan! old Mantuan! Who understandeth thee not, loves thee not. [*hums*] Ut, re, sol, la, mi, fa. [*he glances over Nathaniel's shoulder*] Under pardon, sir, what are the contents? or, rather, as Horace says in his —What, my soul, verses?

Sir Nathaniel. Ay sir, and very learned.

Holofernes. Let me hear a staff, a stanze, a verse. Lege, 110 domine.

Sir Nathaniel [*reads*]. 'If love make me forsworn,
how shall I swear to love?
Ah, never faith could hold, if not to beauty vowed!
Though to myself forsworn, to thee I'll faithful prove.
Those thoughts to me were oaks, to thee like
osiers bowed.
Study his bias leaves, and makes his book thine eyes,
Where all those pleasures live that art
would comprehend:

If knowledge be the mark, to know thee shall suffice.
　　Well learnéd is that tongue, that well can
　　thee commend,
120 All ignorant that soul, that sees thee without wonder—
　　Which is to me some praise that I thy parts admire.
Thy eye Jove's lightning bears, thy voice his
　　dreadful thunder,
　　Which, not to anger bent, is music and
　　sweet fire.
Celestial as thou art, O pardon love this wrong,
That singës heaven's praise with such an earthly tongue!'
　　Holofernes. You find not the apostrophus, and so miss
the accent. Let me supervise the canzonet. [*he takes the
letter*] Here are only numbers ratified, but for the
elegancy, facility, and golden cadence of poesy, caret:
130 Ovidius Naso was the man. And why, indeed, 'Naso,'
but for smelling out the odoriferous flowers of fancy,
the jerks of invention? Imitari is nothing: so doth the
hound his master, the ape his keeper, the tired horse his
rider...But, damosella virgin, was this directed to you?
　　Jaquenetta. Ay sir, from one Monsieur Berowne, one
of the strange queen's lords.
　　Holofernes. I will overglance the superscript: 'To the
snow-white hand of the most beauteous Lady Rosaline'.
　　I will look again on the intellect of the letter, for the
140 nomination of the party writing to the person written
unto:
　　'Your Ladyship's in all desired employment,
　　　　　　　　　　　　　　　BEROWNE.'
Sir Nathaniel, this Berowne is one of the votaries with
the king, and here he hath framed a letter to a sequent
of the stranger queen's: which accidentally, or by the
way of progression, hath miscarried. Trip and go, my
sweet, deliver this paper into the royal hand of the king

—it may concern much: stay not thy complement, I
forgive thy duty—adieu.   150

Jaquenetta. Good Costard go with me...Sir, God
save your life!

Costard. Have with thee, my girl. [*they go off together*

Sir Nathaniel. Sir, you have done this in the fear of
God, very religiously: and, as a certain father saith—

Holofernes. Sir, tell not me of the father, I do fear
colourable colours....But to return to the verses—did
they please you, Sir Nathaniel?

Sir Nathaniel. Marvellous well for the pen.

Holofernes. I do dine to-day at the father's of a certain 160
pupil of mine, where if—before repast—it shall please
you to gratify the table with a grace, I will, on my
privilege I have with the parents of the foresaid child
or pupil, undertake your ben venuto; where I will
prove those verses to be very unlearned, neither savour-
ing of poetry, wit, nor invention. I beseech your society.

Sir Nathaniel. And thank you too: for society—saith
the text—is the happiness of life.

Holofernes. And, certes, the text most infallibly concludes it. [*to Dull*] Sir, I do invite you too, you shall 170
not say me nay: pauca verba. Away, the gentles are at
their game, and we will to our recreation.

[*they depart*

[4. 3.] '*Enter* BEROWNE, *with a paper in his hand, alone*'

Berowne [*reads*]. 'The king he is hunting the deer'...
I am coursing myself....'
They have pitched a toil, I am toiling in a pitch—pitch
that defiles; defile! a foul word. Well, set thee down,
sorrow; for so they say the fool said, and so say I, and I

the fool: well proved, wit! By the Lord, this love is as
mad as Ajax, it kills sheep, it kills me, I a sheep—well
proved again o' my side! I will not love; if I do, hang
me: i'faith I will not. O, but her eye! by this light,
10 but for her eye, I would not love her; yes, for her two
eyes. Well, I do nothing in the world but lie, and lie
in my throat. By heaven, I do love, and it hath taught
me to rhyme, and to be melancholy: and here is part
of my rhyme, and here my melancholy. [*he sighs*]
Well, she hath one o' my sonnets already. The clown
bore it, the fool sent it, and the lady hath it: sweet clown,
sweeter fool, sweetest lady! By the world, I would not
care a pin if the other three were in. Here comes one
with a paper—God give him grace to groan!

[*he climbs into a tree*

The KING *approaches with a paper in his hand*

20 *King* [*groans*]. Ay me!
(*Berowne.* Shot, by heaven! Proceed, sweet Cupid. Thou
hast thumped him with thy birdbolt under the left pap
[*the King warily glances about him*] In faith secrets!
King [*reads*]. 'So sweet a kiss the golden sun gives not
To those fresh morning drops upon the rose,
As thy eye-beams, when their fresh rays have smote
The night of dew that on my cheeks down flows:
Nor shines the silver moon one half so bright
Through the transparent bosom of the deep,
30 As doth thy face through tears of mine give light:
Thou shin'st in every tear that I do weep,
No drop but as a coach doth carry thee:
So ridest thou triumphing in my woe.
Do but behold the tears that swell in me,
And they thy glory through my grief
will show:

But do not love thyself—then thou wilt keep
My tears for glasses, and still make me weep.
O queen of queens, how far dost thou excel
No thought can think, nor tongue of mortal tell.'
How shall she know my griefs? I'll drop the paper. 40
Sweet leaves, shade folly. Who is he comes here?

> [*he hides behind a bush*

*LONGAVILLE comes up, perusing a paper; there is a second
paper in his hat and a third at his belt*

What, Longaville! and reading! listen ear.
  (*Berowne*. Now, in thy likeness, one more fool appear!
Longaville. Ay me! I am forsworn.
  (*Berowne*. Why, he comes in like a perjure, wearing
papers.
  (*King*. In love I hope—sweet fellowship in shame!
  (*Berowne*. One drunkard loves another of the name.
Longaville. Am I the first that have been perjured so?
  (*Berowne*. I could put thee in comfort—not by two
    that I know. 50
Thou makest the triumviry, the corner-cap of society,
The shape of Love's Tyburn, that hangs up Simplicity.
Longaville. I fear these stubborn lines lack power
  to move....
[*reads*] 'O sweet Maria, empress of my love!'
These numbers will I tear, and write in prose.

> [*he tears the paper*

  (*Berowne*. O, rhymes are guards on wanton
    Cupid's hose—
Disfigure not his shop.
Longaville [*plucks the paper from his belt*]. This same
  shall go.

> '*He reads the sonnet*'

'Did not the heavenly rhetoric of thine eye,

'Gainst whom the world cannot hold argument,
60 Persuade my heart to this false perjury?
Vows for thee broke deserve not punishment.
A woman I forswore, but I will prove,
Thou being a goddess, I forswore not thee.
My vow was earthly, thou a heavenly love.
Thy grace being gained cures all disgrace in me.
Vows are but breath, and breath a vapour is.
Then thou, fair sun, which on my earth dost shine,
Exhal'st this vapour-vow—in thee it is:
If broken then, it is no fault of mine:
70 If by me broke, what fool is not so wise
To loose an oath to win a paradise?'
(*Berowne.* This is the liver vein, which makes flesh
   a deity,
A green goose a goddess—pure, pure idolatry.
God amend us, God amend, we are much out o'th'way.
Longaville. By whom shall I send this?—

DUMAINE approaches, with a paper

                    Company! stay. [*he steps aside*
(*Berowne.* All hid, all hid! an old infant play—
Like a demigod here sit I in the sky,
And wretched fools' secrets heedfully o'er-eye.
More sacks to the mill! O heavens, I have my wish—
80 Dumaine transformed, four woodcocks in a dish!
Dumaine. O most divine Kate!
(*Berowne.* O most profane coxcomb!
Dumaine. By heaven, the wonder in a mortal eye!
(*Berowne.* By earth, she is not, corporal, there
   you lie.
Dumaine. Her amber hair for foul hath amber quoted.
(*Berowne.* An amber-coloured raven was well noted.
Dumaine. As upright as the cedar,

(*Berowne*.   Stoop, I say!
Her shoulder is with child.
    Dumaine.   As fair as day!
(*Berowne*. Ay, as some days, but then no sun must shine.
    Dumaine. O that I had my wish!
(*Longaville*.   And I had mine! 90
(*King*. And I mine too, good Lord!
(*Berowne*. Amen, so I had mine. Is not that a
    good word?
    Dumaine. I would forget her, but a fever she
Reigns in my blood, and will rememb'red be.
(*Berowne*. A fever in your blood! why then incision,
Would let her out in saucers—sweet misprision!
    Dumaine. Once more I'll read the ode that I have writ.
(*Berowne*. Once more I'll mark how love can vary wit.

      '*Dumaine reads his sonnet*'

Dumaine. 'On a day, alack the day!
        Love, whose month is ever May,   100
        Spied a blossom passing fair
        Playing in the wanton air:
        Through the velvet leaves the wind,
        All unseen, can passage find;
        That the lover, sick to death,
        Wished himself the heaven's breath.
        Air, quoth he, thy cheeks may blow—
        Air, would I might triumph so.
        But alack, my hand is sworn,
        Ne'er to pluck thee from thy thorn: 110
        Vow, alack, for youth unmeet,
        Youth so apt to pluck a sweet.
        Do not call it sin in me,
        That I am forsworn for thee;
        Thou for whom e'en Jove would swear

Juno but an Ethiope were,
And deny himself for Jove,
Turning mortal for thy love.'
This will I send, and something else more plain.
120 That shall express my true-love's fasting pain.
O, would the King, Berowne, and Longaville,
Were lovers too! Ill, to example ill,
Would from my forehead wipe a perjured note;
For none offend, where all alike do dote.
    Longaville [*advances*]. Dumaine, thy love is far
        from charity,
That in love's grief desir'st society:
You may look pale, but I should blush, I know,
To be o'erheard and taken napping so.
    King [*advances*]. Come sir, you blush; as his your
        case is such;
130 You chide at him, offending twice as much.
You do not love Maria? Longaville
Did never sonnet for her sake compile,
Nor never lay his wreathèd arms athwart
His loving bosom to keep down his heart.
I have been closely shrouded in this bush,
And marked you both, and for you both did blush.
I heard your guilty rhymes, observed your fashion,
Saw sighs reek from you, noted well your passion.
'Ay me,' says one! 'O Jove,' the other cries!
140 One, her hairs were gold, crystal the other's eyes.
    [*to Longaville*] You would for paradise break faith
        and troth—
    [*to Dumaine*] And Jove, for your love, would infringe
        an oath.
What will Berowne say, when that he shall hear
Faith so infringèd, which such zeal did swear?
How will he scorn! how will he spend his wit!

How will he triumph, leap, and laugh at it!
For all the wealth that ever I did see,
I would not have him know so much by me.
  Berowne. Now step I forth to whip hypocrisy....
                  [he descends from the tree
Ah, good my liege, I pray thee, pardon me: 150
Good heart! what grace hast thou, thus to reprove
These worms for loving, that art most in love?
Your eyes do make no coaches; in your tears
There is no certain princess that appears;
You'll not be perjured, 'tis a hateful thing;
Tush, none but minstrels like of sonneting.
But are you not ashamed? nay, are you not,
All three of you, to be thus much o'er-shot?
You found his mote; the king your mote did see;
But I a beam do find in each of three.   160
O, what a scene of fool'ry have I seen,
Of sighs, of groans, of sorrow, and of teen:
O me, with what strict patience have I sat,
To see a king transforméd to a gnat!
To see great Hercules whipping a gig,
And profound Solomon to tune a jig,
And Nestor play at push-pin with the boys,
And critic Timon laugh at idle toys!
Where lies thy grief, O tell me, good Dumaine?
And, gentle Longaville, where lies thy pain?   170
And where my liege's? all about the breast.
A caudle, ho!
  King.   Too bitter is thy jest.
Are we betrayed thus to thy over-view?
  Berowne. Not you to me, but I betrayed by you.
I that am honest, I that hold it sin
To break the vow I am engagéd in,
I am betrayed by keeping company

†With moon-like men, men of inconstancy.
When shall you see me write a thing in rhyme?
180 Or groan for Joan? or spend a minute's time
In pruning me? When shall you hear that I
Will praise a hand, a foot, a face, an eye,
A gait, a state, a brow, a breast, a waist,
A leg, a limb?—
   King.   Soft! Whither away so fast?
A true man or a thief that gallops so?
   Berowne. I post from love, good lover let me go.

     COSTARD and JAQUENETTA approach

   Jaquenetta. God bless the king!
   King.   What present hast thou there?
   Costard. Some certain treason.
   King.   What makes treason here?
   Costard. Nay, it makes nothing, sir.
   King.   If it mar nothing neither,
190 The treason and you go in peace away together.
   Jaquenetta. I beseech your grace, let this letter be read.
                     [*she proffers a paper*
Our Person misdoubts it; 'twas treason, he said.
   King. Berowne, read it over.   ['*he reads the letter*'
                      Where hadst thou it?
   Jaquenetta. Of Costard.
   King. Where hadst thou it?
   Costard. Of Dun Adramadio, Dun Adramadio.
                 [*Berowne tears the letter*
   King. How now, what is in you? why dost thou
     tear it?
   Berowne. A toy my liege, a toy; your grace needs not
     fear it.
   Longaville. It did move him to passion, and therefore
     let's hear it.

Dumaine [*picks up the pieces*]. It is Berowne's writing,
   and here is his name.   200
Berowne [*to Costard*]. Ah, you whoreson loggerhead,
   you were born to do me shame!
Guilty, my lord, guilty! I confess, I confess.
  King. What?
  Berowne. That you three fools lacked me fool to make
   up the mess.
He, he, and you, and you my liege, and I,
Are pick-purses in love, and we deserve to die.
O, dismiss this audience, and I shall tell you more.
  Dumaine. Now the number is even.
  Berowne.   True, true, we are four.
Will these turtles be gone?
  King.   Hence, sirs, away.
  Costard. Walk aside the true folk, and let the
   traitors stay.   210
  [*Costard and Jaquenetta depart lovingly, arm in arm*
  Berowne. Sweet lords, sweet lovers, O let us embrace!
As true we are as flesh and blood can be—
The sea will ebb and flow, heaven show his face;
  Young blood doth not obey an old decree:
We cannot cross the cause why we were born;
Therefore of all hands must we be forsworn.
  King. What, did these rent lines show some love
   of thine?
  Berowne. 'Did they,' quoth you? Who sees the
   heavenly Rosaline,
That, like a rude and savage man of Inde,
  At the first op'ning of the gorgeous east,   220
Bows not his vassal head, and strucken blind,
  Kisses the base ground with obedient breast?
What péremptory eagle-sighted eye
  Dares look upon the heaven of her brow,

That is not blinded by her majesty?
King. What zeal, what fury hath inspired
    thee now?
My love, her mistress, is a gracious moon,
    She, an attending star, scarce seen a light.
Berowne. My eyes are then no eyes, nor I Berowne.
230   O, but for my love, day would turn to night!
Of all complexions the culled sovereignty
    Do meet as at a fair in her fair cheek,
Where several worthies make one dignity,
    Where nothing wants that want itself doth seek.
Lend me the flourish of all gentle tongues—
    Fie, painted rhetoric, O she needs it not,
To things of sale a seller's praise belongs:
    She passes praise—then praise too short doth blot.
A withered hermit, five-score winters worn,
240   Might shake off fifty, looking in her eye:
Beauty doth varnish age, as if new-born,
    And gives the crutch the cradle's infancy.
O, 'tis the sun that maketh all things shine!
King. By heaven, thy love is black as ebony.
Berowne. Is ebony like her? O wood divine!
    A wife of such wood were felicity.
O, who can give an oath? where is a book?
    That I may swear beauty doth beauty lack,
If that she learn not of her eye to look:
250   No face is fair that is not full so black.
King. O paradox! Black is the badge of hell,
    The hue of dungeons and the School of Night—
†A beauty's crest becomes the heavens well!
Berowne. Devils soonest tempt, resembling spirits
    of light.
O, if in black my lady's brows be decked,
    It mourns that painting and usurping hair

Should ravish doters with a false aspéct;
  And therefore is she born to make black fair.
Her favour turns the fashion of the days,
  For native blood is counted painting now;   260
And therefore red, that would avoid dispraise,
  Paints itself black, to imitate her brow.
Dumaine. To look like her are chimney-
  sweepers black.
Longaville. And since her time are colliers
  counted bright.
King. †And Ethiopes their sweet complexion crack.
Dumaine. Dark needs no candles now, for dark
  is light.
Berowne. Your mistresses dare never come in rain,
  For fear their colours should be washed away.
King. 'Twere good, yours did; for sir, to tell you plain,
  I'll find a fairer face not washed to-day.   270
Berowne. I'll prove her fair, or talk till doomsday here.
King. No devil will fright thee then so much as she.
Dumaine. I never knew man hold vile stuff so dear.
Longaville [*thrusts out his boot*]. Look, here's thy love
  —my foot and her face see.
Berowne. O, if the streets were pavéd with thine eyes,
  Her feet were much too dainty for such tread.
Dumaine. O vile! then as she goes what upward lies
  The street should see as she walked overhead.
King. But what of this, are we not all in love?
Berowne. Nothing so sure, and thereby all forsworn.   280
King. Then leave this chat, and good Berowne
  now prove
  Our loving lawful, and our faith not torn.
Dumaine. Ay marry, there—some flattery for this evil.
Longaville. O, some authority how to proceed—
Some tricks, some quillets, how to cheat the devil.

Dumaine. Some salve for perjury.

Berowne.   'Tis more than need.

Have at you then affection's men at arms!

Consider what you first did swear unto:

To fast, to study, and to see no woman;

290 Flat treason 'gainst the kingly state of youth.

Say, can you fast? your stomachs are too young;

And abstinence engenders maladies.

[And where that you have vowed to study, lords,]

In that each of you have forsworn his book,

Can you still dream and pore and thereon look?

For when would you my lord, or you, or you,

Have found the ground of study's excellence

Without the beauty of a woman's face?

From women's eyes this doctrine I derive—

300 They are the ground, the books, the academes,

From whence doth spring the true Promethean fire.

Why, universal plodding prisons up

The nimble spirits in the arteries,

As motion and long-during action tires

The sinewy vigour of the traveller.

Now, for not looking on a woman's face,

You have in that forsworn the use of eyes;

And study too, the causer of your vow.

For where is any author in the world,

310 Teaches such beauty as a woman's eye?

Learning is but an adjunct to ourself,

And where we are our learning likewise is.

Then, when ourselves we see in ladies' eyes,

                        ....with ourselves

[Do we not likewise see our learning there?   ]

O! we have made a vow to study, lords,

And in that vow we have forsworn our books;

For when would you, my liege, or you, or you,

In leaden contemplation have found out
Such fiery numbers as the prompting eyes
Of beauty's tutors have enriched you with?   320
Other slow arts entirely keep the brain;
And therefore, finding barren practisers,
Scarce show a harvest of their heavy toil.
But love, first learnéd in a lady's eyes,
Lives not alone immuréd in the brain;
But with the motion of all elements,
Courses as swift as thought in every power,
And gives to every power a double power,
Above their functions and their offices.
It adds a precious seeing to the eye;   330
A lover's eyes will gaze an eagle blind;
A lover's ear will hear the lowest sound,
†When the suspicious heed of theft is stopped;
Love's feeling is more soft and sensible
Than are the tender horns of cockled snails;
Love's tongue proves dainty Bacchus gross in taste.
For valour, is not Love a Hercules,
Still climbing trees in the Hesperides?
Subtle as Sphinx, as sweet and musical
As bright Apollo's lute, strung with his hair;   340
And, when Love speaks, the voice of all the gods
Make heaven drowsy with the harmony.
Never durst poet touch a pen to write,
Until his ink were temp'red with Love's sighs;
O, then his lines would ravish savage ears,
And plant in tyrants mild humility.
From women's eyes this doctrine I derive:
They sparkle still the right Promethean fire—
They are the books, the arts, the academes,
That show, contain, and nourish all the world;   350
Else none at all in aught proves excellent.

Then fools you were these women to forswear;
Or, keeping what is sworn, you will prove fools.
For wisdom's sake, a word, that all men love;
Or for love's sake, a word that loves all men;
Or for men's sake, the authors of these women;
Or women's sake, by whom we men are men;
Let us once loose our oaths, to find ourselves,
Or else we lose ourselves to keep our oaths.
360 It is religion to be thus forsworn:
For charity itself fulfils the law;
And who can sever love from charity?
   King. Saint Cupid then! and soldiers to the field!
   Berowne. Advance your standards, and upon
     them, lords!
Pell-mell, down with them! but be first advised,
In conflict that you get the sun of them.
   Longaville. Now to plain-dealing; lay these
     glozes by.
Shall we resolve to woo these girls of France?
   King. And win them too. Therefore let us devise
370 Some entertainment for them in their tents.
   Berowne. First from the park let us conduct
     them thither,
Then homeward every man attach the hand
Of his fair mistress. In the afternoon
We will with some strange pastime solace them:
Such as the shortness of the time can shape—
For revels, dances, masks, and merry hours,
Forerun fair Love, strewing her way with flowers.
   King. Away, away! no time shall be omitted,
That will betime, and may by us be fitted.
380 *Berowne.* Allons! Allons! Sowed cockle reaped
     no corn,
   And justice always whirls in equal measure:

Light wenches may prove plagues to men forsworn—
If so, our copper buys no better treasure.

[*they march off*

[5. 1.] HOLOFERNES, SIR NATHANIEL, *and*
DULL *return*

Holofernes. Satis quod sufficit.

Sir Nathaniel. I praise God for you, sir. Your reasons
at dinner have been sharp and sententious; pleasant
without scurrility, witty without affection, audacious
without impudency, learned without opinion, and
strange without heresy. I did converse this quondam
day with a companion of the king's, who is entitled,
nominated, or called, Don Adriano de Armado.

Holofernes. Novi hominem tanquam te. His humour
is lofty, his discourse peremptory: his tongue filed, his 10
eye ambitious, his gait majestical, and his general behaviour vain, ridiculous, and thrasonical. He is too
picked, too spruce, too affected, too odd as it were, too
peregrinate as I may call it.

Sir Nathaniel. A most singular and choice epithet.

[*'draws out his table-book'*
Holofernes. He draweth out the thread of his verbosity
finer than the staple of his argument. I abhor such
fanatical phantasimes, such insociable and point-devise
companions, such rackers of orthography, as to speak
'dout' †sine b, when he should say 'doubt'; 'det,' when 20
he should pronounce 'debt'; d, e, b, t, not d, e, t: he
clepeth a calf 'cauf'; half, 'hauf'; neighbour vocatur
'nebour'; neigh abbreviated 'ne'. This is abhominable
—which he would call abbominable. It insinuateth
me of insania: intelligis ne domine? to make frantic,
lunatic.

Sir Nathaniel. Laus Deo, bone, intelligo.

Holofernes. Bone?—'bone' for 'bene'—Priscian a little scratched—'twill serve.

ARMADO, MOTH *and* COSTARD *come up*

30   *Sir Nathaniel.* Videsne quis venit?

Holofernes. Video, et gaudeo.

Armado. Chirrah!

Holofernes. Quare 'chirrah' not 'sirrah'?

Armado. Men of peace, well encountered.

Holofernes. Most military sir, salutation.

[*they salute with much ceremony, after which Holofernes stands hat in hand*

(*Moth.* They have been at a great feast of languages, and stolen the scraps.

(*Costard.* O, they have lived long on the alms-basket of words! I marvel thy master hath not eaten thee
40   for a word, for thou art not so long by the head as 'honorificabilitudinitatibus': thou art easier swallowed than a flap-dragon.

(*Moth.* Peace! the peal begins.

Armado [*to Holofernes*]. Monsieur, are you not lettered?

Moth. Yes yes, he teaches boys the horn-book. What is a, b, spelt backward with the horn on his head?

Holofernes. Ba, pueritia, with a horn added.

Moth. Ba! most silly sheep with a horn. You hear his learning.

50   *Holofernes.* Quis, quis, thou consonant?

Moth. The last of the five vowels if 'you' repeat them, or the fifth if 'I'.

Holofernes [*with caution*]. I will repeat them, a, e, i—

Moth. The sheep! the other two concludes it—o, u!

Armado. Now by the salt wave of the Mediterraneum,

a sweet touch, a quick venew of wit—snip, snap, quick
and home. It rejoiceth my intellect—true wit.

Moth. Offered by a child to an old man; which is
wit-old.

Holofernes. What is the figure? what is the figure?   60

Moth. Horns!

Holofernes. Thou disputes like an infant: go whip thy
gig.

Moth. Lend me your horn to make one, and I will
whip about your infamy, †manu cita—a gig of a
cuckold's horn!

Costard. An I had but one penny in the world, thou
shouldst have it to buy gingerbread... [*searches his
pocket*] Hold, there is the very remuneration I had of
thy master, thou halfpenny purse of wit, thou pigeon-   70
egg of discretion. O, an the heavens were so pleased
that thou wert but my bastard, what a joyful father
wouldst thou make me! Go to, thou hast it ad dunghill,
at the fingers' ends, as they say.

Holofernes. O, I smell false Latin—'dunghill' for
'unguem'.

Armado [*draws Holofernes aside*]. Arts-man, preambulate. We will be singled from the barbarous....Do
you not educate youth at the charge-house on the top
of the mountain?   80

Holofernes. Or mons, the hill.

Armado. At your sweet pleasure, for the mountain.

Holofernes. I do, sans question.

Armado. Sir, it is the king's most sweet pleasure and
affection to congratulate the princess at her pavilion in
the posteriors of this day, which the rude multitude call
the afternoon.

Holofernes. The posterior of the day, most generous
sir, is liable, congruent, and measurable for the after-

90 noon: the word is well culled, choice, sweet, and apt, I
do assure you sir, I do assure.

Armado. Sir, the king is a noble gentleman, and my
familiar, I do assure ye, very good friend. For what is
inward between us, let it pass, I do beseech thee remember thy courtesy; I beseech thee apparel thy head—
[*Holofernes bows and puts on his hat*]. And among other
importunate and most serious designs, and of great im-
port indeed, too.... But let that pass—for I must tell thee,
it will please his grace (by the world) sometime to lean
100 upon my poor shoulder, and with his royal finger, thus
dally with my excrement, with my mustachio: but sweet
heart, let that pass. By the world, I recount no fable—
some certain special honours it pleaseth his greatness to
impart to Armado, a soldier, a man of travel, that hath
seen the world: but let that pass. The very all of all
is—but, sweet heart, I do implore secrecy—that the king
would have me present the princess (sweet chuck!) with
some delightful ostentation, or show, or pageant, or
antic, or firework. Now, understanding that the curate
110 and your sweet self are good at such eruptions and
sudden breaking out of mirth, as it were, I have ac-
quainted you withal, to the end to crave your assistance.

Holofernes. Sir, you shall present before her the Nine
Worthies.... [*Nathaniel draws nigh*] Sir Nathaniel, as
concerning some entertainment of time, some show in
the posterior of this day, to be rend'red by our assistance, the king's command, and this most gallant,
illustrate, and learned gentleman, before the princess.
I say none so fit as to present the Nine Worthies.

120 *Sir Nathaniel.* Where will you find men worthy
enough to present them?

Holofernes. Joshua yourself, [myself, and] this gallant
gentleman, Judas Maccabæus; this swain, because of

his great limb or joint, shall pass Pompey the great—the
page, Hercules.

Armado. Pardon, sir—error: he is not quantity enough
for that worthy's thumb. He is not so big as the end of
his club.

Holofernes. Shall I have audience? he shall present
Hercules in minority: his 'enter' and 'exit' shall be 130
strangling a snake; and I will have an apology for that
purpose.

Moth. An excellent device! So, if any of the audience
hiss, you may cry, 'Well done, Hercules, now thou
crushest the snake.' That is the way to make an offence
gracious, though few have the grace to do it.

Armado. For the rest of the worthies?

Holofernes. I will play three myself.

Moth. Thrice-worthy gentleman!

Armado. Shall I tell you a thing?   140

Holofernes. We attend.

Armado. We will have, if this fadge not, an antic.
[*he draws him apart; and then turns to the others*]
I beseech you, follow.

Holofernes. Via, goodman Dull! thou hast spoken no
word all this while.

Dull. Nor understood none neither, sir.

Holofernes. Allons! we will employ thee.

Dull. I'll make one in a dance, or so; or I will play
On the tabor to the worthies, and let them dance the hay.

Holofernes. Most dull, honest Dull! to our sport: away! 150
[*Armado and Holofernes depart together; the rest follow*

[5. 2.] *Another part of the Park; before the
pavilion of the Princess*

The PRINCESS, KATHARINE, ROSALINE, *and* MARIA
come from the pavilion

Princess. Sweet hearts, we shall be rich ere we depart,
If fairings come thus plentifully in.
A lady walled about with diamonds!
Look you, what I have from the loving king.
Rosaline. Madam, came nothing else along with that?
Princess. Nothing but this! Yes, as much love in rhyme
As would be crammed up in a sheet of paper
Writ o' both sides the leaf, margent and all—
That he was fain to seal on Cupid's name.
10 *Rosaline.* That was the way to make his godhead wax;
For he hath been five thousand years a boy.
Katharine. Ay, and a shrewd unhappy gallows too.
Rosaline. You'll ne'er be friends with him, a' killed
    your sister.
Katharine. He made her melancholy, sad, and heavy—
And so she died: had she been light, like you,
Of such a merry, nimble, stirring spirit,
She might ha' been a grandam ere she died.
And so may you; for a light heart lives long.
Rosaline. What's your dark meaning, mouse, of this
    light word?
20 *Katharine.* A light condition in a beauty dark.
Rosaline. We need more light to find your meaning out.
Katharine. You'll mar the light by taking it in snuff;
Therefore, I'll darkly end the argument.
Rosaline. Look, what you do, you do it still i'th' dark.
Katharine. So do not you, for you are a light wench.
Rosaline. Indeed I weigh not you, and therefore light.

Katharine. You weigh me not! O, that's you care not
  for me.
Rosaline. Great reason; for, 'past cure is still past care.'
Princess. Well bandied both—a set of wit well played.
But Rosaline, you have a favour too!   30
Who sent it? and what is it?
Rosaline.   I would you knew.
An if my face were but as fair as yours,
My favour were as great—be witness this.
                              [*she shows her fairing*
Nay, I have verses too, I thank Berowne—
The numbers true, and were the numb'ring too,
I were the fairest goddess on the ground.
I am compared to twenty thousand fairs.
O, he hath drawn my picture in his letter!
Princess. Anything like?
Rosaline. Much in the letters, nothing in the praise.   40
Princess. Beauteous as ink: a good conclusion.
Katharine. Fair as a text B in a copy-book.
Rosaline. 'Ware pencils, ho! Le me not die your debtor,
My red dominical, my golden letter.
O, that your face were not so full of O's!
Katharine. A pox of that jest! and I beshrow all
  shrows!
Princess. But what was sent to you from fair Dumaine?
Katharine. Madam, this glove.
Princess.   Did he not send you twain?
Katharine. Yes madam; and, moreover,
Some thousand verses of a faithful lover—   50
A huge translation of hypocrisy,
Vilely compiled, profound simplicity.
Maria. This, and these pearls, to me sent Longaville;
The letter is too long by half a mile.
Princess. I think no less. Dost thou not wish in heart

The chain were longer and the letter short?
Maria. Ay, or I would these hands might
never part.
Princess. We are wise girls to mock our lovers so.
Rosaline. They are worse fools to purchase mocking so.
60 That same Berowne I'll torture ere I go.
O, that I knew he were but in by th' week,
How I would make him fawn, and beg, and seek,
And wait the season, and observe the times,
And spend his prodigal wits in bootless rhymes,
And shape his service wholly to my hests,
And make him proud to make me proud, that jests!
†So planet-like would I o'ersway his state
That he should be my fool, and I his fate.
Princess. None are so surely caught, when they
are catched,
70 As wit turned fool. Folly, in wisdom hatched,
Hath wisdom's warrant, and the help of school,
And wit's own grace to grace a learnéd fool.
Rosaline. The blood of youth burns not with
such excess,
As gravity's revolt to wantonness.
Maria. Folly in fools bears not so strong a note
As fool'ry in the wise, when wit doth dote:
Since all the power thereof it doth apply,
To prove, by wit, worth in simplicity.

BOYET approaches

Princess. Here comes Boyet, and mirth is in his face.
80 *Boyet.* O, I am stabbed with laughter! Where's
her grace?
Princess. Thy news, Boyet?
Boyet.   Prepare, madam, prepare!
Arm, wenches, arm! encounters mounted are

Against your peace. Love doth approach disguised,
Arméd in arguments. You'll be surprised.
Muster your wits, stand in your own defence,
Or hide your heads like cowards and fly hence.
  Princess. Saint Denis to Saint Cupid! What are they,
That charge their breath against us? say, scout, say.
  Boyet. Under the cool shade of a sycamore,
I thought to close mine eyes some half an hour: 90
When lo, to interrupt my purposed rest,
Toward that shade I might behold addrest
The king and his companions: warily
I stole into a neighbour thicket by,
And overheard what you shall overhear—
That, by and by, disguised they will be here.
Their herald is a pretty knavish page,
That well by heart hath conned his embassage.
Action and accent did they teach him there—
'Thus must thou speak', and 'thus thy body bear';   100
And ever and anon they made a doubt
Presence majestical would put him out:
'For,' quoth the king, 'an angel shalt thou see;
Yet fear not thou, but speak audaciously.'
The boy replied, 'An angel is not evil;
I should have feared her had she been a devil.'
With that all laughed, and clapped him on the shoulder,
Making the bold wag by their praises bolder.
One rubbed his elbow thus, and fleered, and swore
A better speech was never spoke before.   110
Another with his finger and his thumb
Cried 'Via! we will do't, come what will come.'
The third he capered and cried, 'All goes well.'
The fourth turned on the toe, and down he fell.
With that they all did tumble on the ground,
With such a zealous laughter so profound,

That in this spleen ridiculous appears,
To check their folly, passion's solemn tears.
   Princess. But what, but what? come they to visit us?
120 *Boyet.* They do, they do; and are apparelled thus,
Like Muscovites or Russians, as I guess.
Their purpose is to parley, court, and dance—
†And every one his love-suit will advance
Unto his several mistress; which they'll know
By favours several which they did bestow.
   Princess. And will they so? the gallants shall be tasked:
For, ladies, we will every one be masked,
And not a man of them shall have the grace,
Despite of suit, to see a lady's face.
130 Hold Rosaline, this favour thou shalt wear,
And then the king will court thee for his dear;
Hold, take thou this my sweet, and give me thine,
So shall Berowne take me for Rosaline.
                 [they change favours
And change you favours too, so shall your loves
Woo contrary, deceived by these removes.
   Rosaline. Come on then, wear the favours most
     in sight.
   Katharine. But in this changing what is your intent?
   Princess. The effect of my intent is to cross theirs:
They do it but in mockery-merriment,
140 And mock for mock is only my intent.
Their several counsels they unbosom shall
To loves mistook, and so be mocked withal
Upon the next occasion that we meet,
With visages displayed, to talk and greet.
   Rosaline. But shall we dance, if they desire us to't?
   Princess. No, to the death, we will not move a foot—
Nor to their penned speech render we no grace;
But while 'tis spoke each turn away her face.

Boyet. Why, that contempt will kill the speaker's heart,
And quite divorce his memory from his part.   150
Princess. Therefore I do it, and I make no doubt
The rest will e'er come in, if he be out.
There's no such sport as sport by sport o'erthrown,
To make theirs ours and ours none but our own:
So shall we stay, mocking intended game,
And they, well mocked, depart away with shame.

[a trumpet

Boyet. The trumpet sounds! be masked, the
    maskers come.   [*the ladies don their vizards*

'*Enter Blackamoors with music, the Boy with a speech, and
the rest of the Lords disguised*' *and masked as Russians*

Moth. 'All hail, the richest beauties on the earth'—
Boyet. Beauties no richer than rich taffeta.
Moth. 'A holy parcel of the fairest dames,   160

    '*The ladies turn their backs to him*'

That ever turned their backs to mortal views!'
Berowne. 'Their eyes,' villain, 'their eyes.'
Moth. 'That ever turned their eyes to mortal views.
Out—'
Boyet. True, 'out' indeed.
Moth. 'Out of your favours, heavenly spirits, vouchsafe
Not to behold—'
Berowne. 'Once to behold,' rogue.
Moth. 'Once to behold with your sun-beaméd eyes,
        —with your sun-beaméd eyes—' 170
Boyet. They will not answer to that epithet—
You were best call it 'daughter-beaméd eyes.'
Moth. They do not mark me, and that brings me out.
Berowne. Is this your perfectness? be gone you rogue.

[Moth flies from the presence

Rosaline [*turns, showing the favour of the Princess*].
What would these strangers? Know their minds, Boyet.
If they do speak our language, 'tis our will
That some plain man recount their purposes.
Know what they would.

    Boyet.   What would you with the princess?
    Berowne. Nothing but peace and gentle visitation.
180 *Rosaline.* What would they, say they?
    Boyet. Nothing but peace and gentle visitation.
    Rosaline. Why, that they have—and bid them so
      be gone.
    Boyet. She says you have it, and you may be gone.
    King. Say to her we have measured many miles
To tread a measure with her on this grass.
    Boyet. They say that they have measured many a mile,
To tread a measure with you on this grass.
    Rosaline. It is not so! Ask them how many inches
Is in one mile. If they have measured many,
190 The measure then of one is eas'ly told.
    Boyet. If to come hither you have measured miles,
And many miles, the princess bids you tell
How many inches doth fill up one mile.
    Berowne. Tell her we measure them by weary steps.

The ladies advance

    Boyet. She hears herself.
    Rosaline.   How many weary steps,
Of many weary miles you have o'ergone,
Are numb'red in the travel of one mile?
    Berowne. We number nothing that we spend for you—
Our duty is so rich, so infinite,
200 That we may do it still without account.
Vouchsafe to show the sunshine of your face,
That we—like savages—may worship it.

Rosaline. My face is but a moon, and clouded too.

King. Blesséd are clouds, to do as such clouds do.
Vouchsafe bright moon, and these thy stars to shine—
Those clouds removed—upon our watery eyne.

Rosaline. O vain petitioner, beg a greater matter—
Thou now requests but moonshine in the water.

King. Then, in our measure, do but vouchsafe
   one change.
Thou bid'st me beg—this begging is not strange.   210

Rosaline. Play music then! nay, you must do it soon!
Not yet?—no dance! Thus change I like the moon.

King. Will you not dance? How come you
   thus estranged?

Rosaline. You took the moon at full, but now
   she's changed!   [*the musicians strike up*

King. Yet still she is the Moon, and I the Man.
The music plays—vouchsafe some motion to it.

Rosaline. Our ears vouchsafe it.

King.   But your legs should do it.

Rosaline. Since you are strangers, and come here
   by chance,
We'll not be nice—take hands—We will not dance.

King. Why take we hands then?

Rosaline.   Only to part friends. 220
[*to the ladies*] Curtsy sweethearts, and so the
   measure ends.   [*they curtsy*

King. More measure of this measure—be not nice.

Rosaline. We can afford no more at such a price.

King. Price you yourselves. What buys
   your company?

Rosaline. Your absence only.

King.   That can never be.

Rosaline. Then cannot we be bought: and so adieu—
Twice to your visor, and half once to you!

King. If you deny to dance, let's hold more chat.
Rosaline. In private then.
King.   I am best pleased with that.

> [*they talk apart*

230 *Berowne.* White-handed mistress, one sweet word
    with thee.
Princess. Honey, and milk, and sugar; there is three.
Berowne. Nay then, two treys—an if you grow so nice—
Metheglin, wort, and malmsey; well run, dice!
There's half-a-dozen sweets.
Princess.   Seventh sweet, adieu!
Since you can cog, I'll play no more with you.
Berowne. One word in secret.
Princess.   Let it not be sweet.
Berowne. Thou grievest my gall.
Princess.   Gall? bitter.
Berowne.   Therefore meet.

> [*they talk apart*

Dumaine. Will you vouchsafe with me to change
    a word?
Maria. Name it.
Dumaine.   Fair lady,—
Maria.   Say you so? Fair lord,—
240 Take that for your fair lady.
Dumaine.   Please it you,
As much in private, and I'll bid adieu.

> [*they talk apart*

Katharine. What, was your vizard made without
    a tongue?
Longaville. I know the reason, lady, why you ask.
Katharine. O, for your reason! quickly, sir—I long.
Longaville. You have a double tongue within
    your mask,
And would afford my speechless vizard half.

Katharine. 'Veal' quoth the Dutchman. Is not 'veal'
  a calf?
Longaville. A calf, fair lady?
Katharine.   No, a fair lord calf.
Longaville. Let's part the word.
Katharine.   No, I'll not be your half:
Take all and wean it—it may prove an ox.   250
Longaville. Look how you butt yourself in these
  sharp mocks.
Will you give horns, chaste lady? do not so.
Katharine. Then die a calf, before your horns do grow.
Longaville. One word in private with you ere I die.
Katharine. Bleat softly then, the butcher hears
  you cry.   [*they talk apart*
Boyet. The tongues of mocking wenches are
  as keen
  As is the razor's edge invisible,
Cutting a smaller hair than may be seen:
  Above the sense of sense: so sensible
Seemeth their conference, their conceits have wings, 260
Fleeter than arrows, bullets, wind, thought,
  swifter things.
Rosaline [*suddenly*]. Not one word more my maids,
  break off, break off.

  The ladies swiftly turn from their partners

Berowne. By heaven, all dry-beaten with pure scoff!
King. Farewell mad wenches, you have simple wits.
Princess. Twenty adieus, my frozen Muscovits.

    The King departs with his train

Are these the breed of wits so wondered at?
Boyet. Tapers they are with your sweet breaths
  puffed out.

Rosaline. Well-liking wits they have—gross gross,
    fat fat.
Princess. O poverty in wit, kingly-poor flout!
270 Will they not, think you, hang themselves to-night?
    Or ever but in vizards show their faces?
This pert Berowne was out of count'nance quite.
Rosaline. O, they were all in lamentable cases!
The king was weeping-ripe for a good word.
Princess. Berowne did swear himself out of all suit.
Maria. Dumaine was at my service, and his sword.
'No point,' quoth I—my servant straight was mute.
Katharine. Lord Longaville said I came o'er his heart:
And trow you what he called me?
    Princess.   Qualm, perhaps.
280 *Katharine.* Yes, in good faith.
    Princess.   Go, sickness as thou art.
Rosaline. Well, better wits have worn plain statute-caps.
But will you hear? the king is my love sworn.
Princess. And quick Berowne hath plighted faith
    to me.
Katharine. And Longaville was for my service born.
Maria. Dumaine is mine as sure as bark on tree.
Boyet. Madam, and pretty mistresses, give ear.
Immediately they will again be here
In their own shapes; for it can never be
They will digest this harsh indignity.
290 *Princess.* Will they return?
    Boyet.   They will, they will, God knows;
And leap for joy, though they are lame with blows:
Therefore change favours, and when they repair,
Blow like sweet roses in this summer air.
Princess. How blow? how blow? speak to
    be understood.
Boyet. Fair ladies, masked, are roses in their bud:

Dismasked, their damask sweet commixture shown,
Are angels vailing clouds, or roses blown.
　Princess. Avaunt, perplexity! What shall we do
If they return in their own shapes to woo?
　Rosaline. Good madam, if by me you'll be advised,　300
Let's mock them still as well known as disguised:
Let us complain to them what fools were here,
Disguised like Muscovites, in shapeless gear;
And wonder what they were, and to what end
Their shallow shows and prologue vilely penned,
And their rough carriage so ridiculous,
Should be presented at our tent to us.
　Boyet. Ladies, withdraw; the gallants are at hand.
　Princess. Whip to our tents as roes run o'er the land.
　　　　　　　　　　　　　　　　　[they do so

The KING, BEROWNE, LONGAVILLE, and DUMAINE,
return in their proper habits

　King. Fair sir, God save you! where's the princess?　310
　Boyet. Gone to her tent. Please it your majesty,
Command me any service to her thither?
　King. That she vouchsafe me audience for one word.
　Boyet. I will, and so will she, I know, my lord.
　　　　　　　　　　　　　　　[he enters the tent
　Berowne. This fellow pecks up wit, as pigeons pease,
And utters it again when God doth please.
He is Wit's pedler, and retails his wares
At wakes and wassails, meetings, markets, fairs:
And we that sell by gross, the Lord doth know,
Have not the grace to grace it with such show.　320
This gallant pins the wenches on his sleeve.
Had he been Adam, he had tempted Eve.
A' can carve too, and lisp: why, this is he
That kissed his hand away in courtesy.

This is the ape of form, monsieur the nice,
That when he plays at tables chides the dice
In honourable terms; nay, he can sing
A mean most meanly, and, in ushering,
Mend him who can. The ladies call him sweet.
330 The stairs as he treads on them kiss his feet.
This is the flower that smiles on every one,
To show his teeth as white as whalës-bone.
And consciences that will not die in debt
Pay him the due of honey-tongued Boyet.
  King. A blister on his sweet tongue, with my heart,
That put Armado's page out of his part.

*The ladies come from the pavilion, unmasked and with
their own favours; BOYET ushering the PRINCESS*

  Berowne. See where it comes! Behaviour, what
    wert thou
Till this man showed thee? and what art thou now?
  King. All hail sweet madam, and fair time of day!
340 *Princess.* 'Fair' in 'all hail' is foul, as I conceive.
  King. Construe my speeches better, if you may.
  Princess. Then wish me better, I will give
    you leave.
  King. We came to visit you, and purpose now
    To lead you to our court—vouchsafe it then.
  Princess. This field shall hold me, and so hold
    your vow:
    Nor God nor I delights in perjured men.
  King. Rebuke me not for that which you provoke:
    The virtue of your eye must break my oath.
  Princess. You nickname virtue—'vice' you should
    have spoke;
350   For virtue's office never breaks men's troth.
Now by my maiden honour, yet as pure

As the unsullied lily, I protest,
A world of torments though I should endure,
    I would not yield to be your house's guest:
So much I hate a breaking cause to be
Of heavenly oaths vowed with integrity.
    King. O, you have lived in desolation here,
        Unseen, unvisited, much to our shame.
    Princess. Not so my lord, it is not so, I swear.

    We have had pastimes here and pleasant game.   360
A mess of Russians left us but of late.
    King. How madam? Russians?
    Princess.   Ay, in truth my lord;
Trim gallants, full of courtship and of state.
    Rosaline. Madam speak true. It is not so my lord.
My lady, to the manner of the days,
In courtesy gives undeserving praise.
We four indeed confronted were with four
In Russian habit: here they stayed an hour,
And talked apace; and in that hour, my lord,
They did not bless us with one happy word.   370
I dare not call them fools; but this I think,
When they are thirsty, fools would fain have drink.
    Berowne. This jest is dry to me. My gentle sweet,
Your wit makes wise things foolish: when we greet,
With eyes best seeing, heaven's fiery eye,
By light we lose light; your capacity
Is of that nature that to your huge store
Wise things seem foolish and rich things but poor.
    Rosaline. This proves you wise and rich; for in
        my eye—
    Berowne. I am a fool, and full of poverty.   380
    Rosaline. But that you take what doth to you belong,
It were a fault to snatch words from my tongue.
    Berowne. O, I am yours, and all that I possess.

6

Rosaline. All the fool mine?

Berowne.   I cannot give you less.

Rosaline. Which of the vizards was it that you wore?

Berowne. Where, when, what vizard? why demand
   you this?

Rosaline. There, then, that vizard—that super-
   fluous case

That hid the worse and showed the better face.

   (*King.* We were descried, they'll mock us
   now downright.

390 (*Dumaine.* Let us confess, and turn it to a jest.

Princess. Amazed, my lord? Why looks your
   highness sad?

Rosaline. Help, hold his brows! he'll swoon! Why
   look you pale?

Sea-sick, I think, coming from Muscovy.

Berowne. Thus pour the stars down plagues
   for perjury.

Can any face of brass hold longer out?

Here stand I, lady—dart thy skill at me,
   Bruise me with scorn, confound me with a flout,

Thrust thy sharp wit quite through my ignorance,
   Cut me to pieces with thy keen conceit,

400 And I will wish thee never more to dance,
   Nor never more in Russian habit wait.

O, never will I trust to speeches penned,
   Nor to the motion of a schoolboy's tongue,

Nor never come in vizard to my friend,
   Nor woo in rhyme, like a blind harper's song.

Taffeta phrases, silken terms precise,
   Three-piled hyperboles, spruce affectation,

Figures pedantical—these summer-flies
   Have blown me full of maggot ostentation.

410 I do forswear them, and I here protest,

By this white glove (how white the hand,
  God knows!)
Henceforth my wooing mind shall be expressed
  In russet yeas and honest kersey noes.
And, to begin, wench—so God help me, la!—
My love to thee is sound, sans crack or flaw.
  Rosaline. Sans 'sans,' I pray you.
  Berowne.   Yet I have a trick
Of the old rage; bear with me, I am sick—
I'll leave it by degrees. Soft, let us see;
Write 'Lord have mercy on us' on those three.
They are infected, in their hearts it lies;   420
They have the plague, and caught it of your eyes.
These lords are visited; you are not free,
For the Lord's tokens on you do I see.
  Princess. No, they are free that gave these tokens
    to us.
  Berowne. Our states are forfeit, seek not to undo us.
  Rosaline. It is not so. For how can this be true,
That you stand forfeit, being those that sue?
  Berowne. Peace! for I will not have to do with you.
  Rosaline. Nor shall not, if I do as I intend.
  Berowne. Speak for yourselves, my wit is at an end. 430
  King. Teach us, sweet madam, for our
    rude transgression
Some fair excuse.
  Princess.   The fairest is confession.
Were you not here but even now, disguised?
  King. Madam, I was.
  Princess.   And were you well advised?
  King. I was, fair madam.
  Princess.   When you then were here,
What did you whisper in your lady's ear?
  King. That more than all the world I did respect her.

                                      6-2

Princess. When she shall challenge this, you will
reject her.

King. Upon mine honour, no.

Princess.   Peace, peace, forbear;
440 Your oath once broke, you force not to forswear.

King. Despise me when I break this oath of mine.

Princess. I will, and therefore keep it....Rosaline,
What did the Russian whisper in your ear?

Rosaline. Madam, he swore that he did hold me dear
As precious eyesight, and did value me
Above this world: adding thereto, moreover,
That he would wed me, or else die my lover.

Princess. God give thee joy of him! the noble lord
Most honourably doth uphold his word.

450 *King.* What mean you, madam? by my life, my troth,
I never swore this lady such an oath.

Rosaline. By heaven you did; and to confirm it plain,
You gave me this....[*she shows a ring*] but take it,
sir, again.

King. My faith and this the princess I did give,
I knew her by this jewel on her sleeve.

Princess. Pardon me sir, this jewel did she wear,
And Lord Berowne (I thank him!) is my dear.
What, will you have me, or your pearl again?

Berowne. Neither of either: I remit both twain.
460 I see the trick on't: here was a consent—
Knowing aforehand of our merriment—
To dash it like a Christmas comedy:
Some carry-tale, some please-man, some slight zany,
Some mumble-news, some trencher-knight, some Dick,
That smiles his cheek in years, and knows the trick
To make my lady laugh, when she's disposed,
Told our intents before; which once disclosed,
The ladies did change favours; and then we,

Following the signs, wooed but the sign of she.
Now to our perjury to add more terror,   470
We are again forsworn, in will and error.
Much upon this 'tis! [*to Boyet*] And might
    not you
Forestall our sport, to make us thus untrue?
Do not you know my lady's foot by th' square,
    And laugh upon the apple of her eye?
And stand between her back, sir, and the fire,
    Holding a trencher, jesting merrily?
You put our page out: go, you are allowed!
Die when you will, a smock shall be your shroud.
You leer upon me, do you? there's an eye   480
Wounds like a leaden sword.
    Boyet.   Full merrily
Hath this brave manage, this career, been run.
    Berowne. Lo, he is tilting straight. Peace, I have done.

COSTARD *comes up*

Welcome, pure wit! thou partest a fair fray.
    Costard. O Lord, sir, they would know
Whether the three Worthies shall come in or no.
    Berowne. What, are there but three?
    Costard.   No sir, but it is vara fine,
For every one pursents three.
    Berowne.   And three times thrice is nine.
    Costard. Not so, sir—under correction, sir—I hope it
    is not so.
You cannot beg us, sir, I can assure you, sir; we know
    what we know: 490
I hope, sir, three times thrice, sir—
    Berowne. Is not nine.
    Costard. Under correction, sir, we know whereuntil
it doth amount.

Berowne. By Jove, I always took three threes for nine.

Costard. O Lord, sir, it were a pity you should get your living by reck'ning, sir.

Berowne. How much is it?

Costard. O Lord, sir, the parties themselves, the actors, 500 sir, will show whereuntil it doth amount: for mine own part, I am, as they say, but to parfect one man in one poor man—Pompion the Great, sir.

Berowne. Art thou one of the Worthies?

Costard. It pleased them to think me worthy of Pompey the Great: for mine own part I know not the degree of the Worthy, but I am to stand for him.

Berowne. Go bid them prepare.

Costard. We will turn it finely off sir, we will take some care.   [*he goes*

King. Berowne, they will shame us: let them not approach.

510 *Berowne.* We are shame-proof, my lord: and 'tis some policy
To have one show worse than the King's and his company.

King. I say they shall not come.

Princess. Nay, my good lord, let me o'errule you now,
That sport best pleases that doth least know how:
Where zeal strives to content, and the contents
Dies in the zeal of that which it presents:
There form confounded makes most form in mirth,
When great things labouring perish in their birth.

Berowne. A right description of our sport, my lord.

Armado appears

520 *Armado.* Anointed, I implore so much expense of thy royal sweet breath as will utter a brace of words.
[*he talks apart with the King, and delivers him a paper*

Princess. Doth this man serve God?

Berowne. Why ask you?

Princess. A' speaks not like a man of God his making.

Armado. That is all one, my fair, sweet honey monarch: for, I protest, the schoolmaster is exceeding fantastical—too-too vain, too-too vain: but we will put it, as they say, to fortuna de la guerra. I wish you the peace of mind, most royal couplement!

> [*he bows low and departs*

King [*cons the paper*]. Here is like to be a good 530 presence of Worthies. He presents Hector of Troy, the swain Pompey the Great, the parish curate Alexander, Armado's page Hercules, the pedant Judas Maccabæus. [*he reads*
'And if these four worthies in their first show thrive,
These four will change habits, and present the
    other five.'

Berowne. There is five in the first show.

King. You are deceived, 'tis not so.

Berowne. The pedant, the braggart, the hedge-priest, the fool, and the boy— 540
Abate throw at novum, and the whole world again
Cannot pick out five such, take each one in
    his vein.

King. The ship is under sail, and here she
    comes amain.

> [*attendants bring seats for the King and the Princess*

> *Enter* COSTARD *armed, for Pompey;*
> *he trips on his sword and falls*

Costard [*prone*]. 'I Pompey am'—

Berowne.   You lie, you are not he.

Costard [*rising*]. 'I Pompey am'—

Boyet.   With libbard's head on knee.

Berowne. Well said old mocker, I must needs be friends
with thee.

Costard. 'I Pompey am, Pompey surnamed the Big'—

Dumaine. The Great.

Costard. It is 'great,' sir.—'Pompey surnamed
the Great,

550 That oft in field with targe and shield did make my foe
to sweat,

And travelling along this coast I here am come by chance,

And lay my arms before the legs of this sweet lass
of France.'   [*he casts down his shield and sword*

If your ladyship would say, 'Thanks Pompey,' I
had done.

Princess. Great thanks, Great Pompey.

Costard. 'Tis not so much worth; but I hope I was
perfect. I made a little fault in 'Great.'

Berowne. My hat to a halfpenny, Pompey proves the
best Worthy.

Enter SIR NATHANIEL *armed, for Alexander*

Sir Nathaniel. 'When in the world I lived, I was the
world's commander:

By east, west, north, and south, I spread my
conquering might:

560 My scutcheon plain declares that I am Alisander.'

Boyet. Your nose says, no, you are not; for it stands
too right.

Berowne. Your nose smells 'no' in this, most tender-
smelling knight.

Princess. The conqueror is dismayed. Proceed,
good Alexander.

Sir Nathaniel. 'When in the world I lived, I was the
world's commander,'—

Boyet. Most true, 'tis right; you were so, Alisander.

Berowne. Pompey the Great,—

Costard. Your servant, and Costard.

Berowne. Take away the conqueror, take away Alisander.

Costard [*to Sir Nathaniel*]. O, sir, you have over- 570
thrown Alisander the conqueror! You will be scraped
out of the painted cloth for this. Your lion, that holds
his poll-axe sitting on a close-stool, will be given to
Ajax—he will be the ninth Worthy. A conqueror, and
afeard to speak! run away for shame, Alisander. [*Sir
Nathaniel departs discomfited*] There, an't shall please
you, a foolish mild man—an honest man, look you, and
soon dashed. He is a marvellous good neighbour, faith,
and a very good bowler: but for Alisander, alas you
see how 'tis—a little o'erparted. But there are Worthies 580
a-coming will speak their mind in some other sort.

Princess. Stand aside, good Pompey.

[*Costard departs*

Enter HOLOFERNES, *for Judas, and*
MOTH, *for Hercules*

Holofernes. 'Great Hercules is presented by this imp,
    Whose club killed Cerberus, that three-
        headed Canis,
And when he was a babe, a child, a shrimp,
    Thus did he strangle serpents in his manus.
Quoniam he seemeth in minority,
Ergo I come with this apology'.
Keep some state in thy exit, and vanish.

[*Moth departs* 590

'Judas I am,'—

Dumaine. A Judas!

Holofernes. Not Iscariot, sir.

'Judas I am, ycliped Maccabæus.'

Dumaine. Judas Maccabæus clipt is plain Judas.

Berowne. A kissing traitor. How, art thou proved Judas?

Holofernes. 'Judas I am,'—

Dumaine. The more shame for you, Judas.

Holofernes. What mean you, sir?

600 *Boyet.* To make Judas hang himself.

Holofernes. Begin sir, you are my elder.

Berowne. Well followed. Judas was hanged on an elder.

Holofernes. I will not be put out of countenance.

Berowne. Because thou hast no face.

Holofernes. What is this?

Boyet. A cittern-head.

Dumaine. The head of a bodkin.

Berowne. A death's face in a ring.

610 *Longaville.* The face of an old Roman coin, scarce seen.

Boyet. The pummel of Cæsar's falchion.

Dumaine. The carved-bone face on a flask.

Berowne. St George's half-cheek in a brooch.

Dumaine. Ay, and in a brooch of lead.

Berowne. Ay, and worn in the cap of a tooth-drawer. And now forward, for we have put thee in countenance.

Holofernes. You have put me out of countenance.

Berowne. False—we have given thee faces.

620 *Holofernes.* But you have out-faced them all.

Berowne. An thou wert a lion, we would do so.

Boyet. Therefore, as he is an ass, let him go. And so adieu, sweet Jude! Nay, why dost thou stay?

Dumaine. For the latter end of his name.

Berowne. For the ass to the Jude: give it him— Jud-as, away.

Holofernes. This is not generous, not gentle,
    not humble.
Boyet. A light for Monsieur Judas! it grows dark, he
    may stumble.   *[Holofernes retires*
Princess. Alas, poor Maccabæus, how hath he
    been baited!

    Enter ARMADO armed, for Hector

Berowne. Hide thy head, Achilles—here comes Hector
in arms.   630
Dumaine. Though my mocks come home by me, I
will now be merry.
King. Hector was but a Troyan in respect of this.
Boyet. But is this Hector?
King. I think Hector was not so clean-timbered.
Longaville. His leg is too big for Hector's.
Dumaine. More calf, certain.
Boyet. No, he is best indued in the small.
Berowne. This cannot be Hector.
Dumaine. He's a god or a painter; for he makes 640
faces.
Armado. 'The armipotent Mars, of lances
    the almighty,
Gave Hector a gift,'—
Dumaine. A gilt nutmeg.
Berowne. A lemon.
Longaville. Stuck with cloves.
Dumaine. No, cloven.
Armado. Peace!
'The armipotent Mars, of lances the almighty,
    Gave Hector a gift, the heir of Ilion,   650
A man so breathed, that certain he would fight ye,
    From morn till night, out of his pavilion.
I am that flower,'—

Dumaine.   That mint.

Longaville.   That columbine.

Armado. Sweet Lord Longaville, rein thy tongue.

Longaville. I must rather give it the rein; for it runs against Hector.

Dumaine. Ay, and Hector's a greyhound.

Armado. The sweet war-man is dead and rotten—
660 sweet chucks, beat not the bones of the buried: when he breathed, he was a man. But I will forward with my device. [*to the Princess*] Sweet royalty, bestow on me the sense of hearing.   ['*Berowne steps forth*'

Princess. Speak brave Hector, we are much delighted.

Armado. I do adore thy sweet grace's slipper.

(*Boyet.* Loves her by the foot.

(*Dumaine.* He may not by the yard.

Armado. 'This Hector far surmounted Hannibal. The party is gone'...

CostARD *returns, with* BEROWNE *following*

670 *Costard.* Fellow Hector, she is gone; she is two months on her way.

Armado. What meanest thou?

Costard. Faith, unless you play the honest Troyan, the poor wench is cast away: she's quick—the child brags in her belly already: 'tis yours.

Armado. Dost thou infamonize me among potentates? thou shalt die.

Costard. Then shall Hector be whipped for Jaquenetta that is quick by him, and hanged for Pompey that is
680 dead by him.

Dumaine. Most rare Pompey!

Boyet. Renowned Pompey!

Berowne. Greater than great, great, great, great Pompey! Pompey the Huge!

Dumaine. Hector trembles.

Berowne. Pompey is moved. More Ates, more Ates! stir them on! stir them on!

Dumaine. Hector will challenge him.

Berowne. Ay, if a' have no more man's blood in's belly than will sup a flea.   690

Armado. By the north pole, I do challenge thee.

Costard. I will not fight with a pole like a northren man; I'll slash, I'll do it by the sword. [*to the Princess*] I bepray you let me borrow my arms again.

                    [*he takes up the sword and shield*

Dumaine. Room for the incensed Worthies.

Costard. I'll do it in my shirt.   [*he strips off his coat*

Dumaine. Most resolute Pompey!

Moth. Master, let me take you a button-hole lower. Do you not see Pompey is uncasing for the combat? What mean you? you will lose your reputation.   700

Armado. Gentlemen, and soldiers, pardon me, I will not combat in my shirt.

Dumaine. You may not deny it, Pompey hath made the challenge.

Armado. Sweet bloods, I both may and will.

Berowne. What reason have you for't?

Armado. The naked truth of it is, I have no shirt. I go woolward for penance.

Moth. True, and it was enjoined him in Rome for want of linen: since when, I'll be sworn, he wore none 710 but a dish-clout of Jaquenetta's, and that a' wears next his heart for a favour.

Monsieur MERCADÉ, *a messenger, comes up*

Mercadé [*bows*]. God save you, madam!

Princess.   Welcome, Mercadé, But that thou interrupt'st our merriment.

Mercadé. I am sorry, madam—for the news I bring,
Is heavy in my tongue. The king your father—
Princess. Dead, for my life!
Mercadé.   Even so; my tale is told.
Berowne. Worthies, away! the scene begins to cloud.
Armado. For mine own part, I breathe free breath:
720 I have seen the day of wrong through the little hole of
discretion, and I will right myself like a soldier.
                              [*the Worthies depart*
King. How fares your majesty?
Princess. Boyet, prepare—I will away to-night.
King. Madam, not so—I do beseech you stay.
Princess. Prepare, I say. I thank you,
        gracious lords,
For all your fair endeavours, and entreat,
Out of a new-sad soul, that you vouchsafe
In your rich wisdom to excuse, or hide,
The liberal opposition of our spirits,
730 If over-boldly we have borne ourselves
In the converse of breath—your gentleness
Was guilty of it. Farewell, worthy lord:
A heavy heart bears not a nimble tongue.
Excuse me so, coming too short of thanks
For my great suit so easily obtained.
  King. The extreme parts of time extremely forms
All causes to the purpose of his speed;
And often, at his very loose, decides
That which long process could not arbitrate.
740 And though the mourning brow of progeny
Forbid the smiling courtesy of love
The holy suit which fain it would convince,
Yet since love's argument was first on foot,
Let not the cloud of sorrow justle it
From what it purposed—since to wail friends lost

Is not by much so wholesome-profitable
As to rejoice at friends but newly found.
  Princess. I understand you not—my griefs
    are double.
  Berowne. Honest plain words best pierce the ear
    of grief—
†And by these bodges understand the king.   750
For your fair sakes have we neglected time,
Played foul-play with our oaths. Your beauty, ladies,
Hath much deformed us, fashioning our humours
Even to the opposéd end of our intents:
And what in us hath seemed ridiculous—
As love is full of unbefitting strains,
All wanton as a child, skipping and vain,
Formed by the eye, and therefore, like the eye
Full of straying shapes, of habits and of forms,
Varying in subjects as the eye doth roll   760
To every varied object in his glance:
Which parti-coated presence of loose love
Put on by us, if, in your heavenly eyes,
Have misbecomed our oaths and gravities,
Those heavenly eyes, that look into these faults,
Suggested us to make. Therefore, ladies,
Our love being yours, the error that love makes
Is likewise yours: we to ourselves prove false,
By being once false for ever to be true
To those that make us both—fair ladies, you.   770
And even that falsehood, in itself a sin,
Thus purifies itself and turns to grace.
  Princess. We have received your letters, full of love;
Your favours, the ambassadors of love;
And in our maiden council rated them
At courtship, pleasant jest, and courtesy,
As bombast and as lining to the time:

But more devout than this in our respects
Have we not been, and therefore met your loves
780 In their own fashion, like a merriment.
    Dumaine. Our letters, madam, showed much more
       than jest.
    Longaville. So did our looks.
    Rosaline.   We did not quote them so.
    King. Now, at the latest minute of the hour,
Grant us your loves.
    Princess.   A time methinks too short
To make a world-without-end bargain in:
No no, my lord, your grace is perjured much,
Full of dear guiltiness; and therefore this—
If for my love (as there is no such cause)
You will do aught, this shall you do for me:
790 Your oath I will not trust, but go with speed
To some forlorn and naked hermitage,
Remote from all the pleasures of the world;
There stay until the twelve celestial signs
Have brought about the annual reckoning.
If this austere insociable life
Change not your offer made in heat of blood,
If frosts and fasts, hard lodging and thin weeds,
Nip not the gaudy blossoms of your love,
But that it bear this trial and last love:
800 Then, at the expiration of the year,
Come challenge me, challenge by these deserts,
And by this virgin palm now kissing thine,
I will be thine; and till that instant shut
My woeful self up in a mourning house,
Raining the tears of lamentation
For the remembrance of my father's death.
If this thou do deny, let our hands part,
Neither entitled in the other's heart.

King. If this, or more than this, I would deny,
To flatter up these powers of mine with rest,   810
The sudden hand of death close up mine eye!
Hence hermit, then—my heart is in thy breast.
                              [they talk apart
[*Berowne.* And what to me, my love? and what   ]
    to me?
†*Rosaline.* You must be purgéd too; your sins are rank.
You are attaint with faults and perjury;
Therefore if you my favour mean to get,
A twelvemonth shall you spend, and never rest,
⌊But seek the weary beds of people sick.   ⌋
    Dumaine. But what to me, my love? but what to me?
A wife?
    Katharine. A beard, fair health, and honesty—   820
With three-fold love I wish you all these three.
    Dumaine. O, shall I say, I thank you gentle wife?
    Katharine. Not so my lord, a twelvemonth and a day
I'll mark no words that smooth-faced wooers say.
Come when the king doth to my lady come;
Then if I have much love, I'll give you some.
    Dumaine. I'll serve thee true and faithfully till then.
    Katharine. Yet swear not, lest ye be forsworn again.
                              [they talk apart
Longaville. What says Maria?
Maria.   At the twelvemonth's end,
I'll change my black gown for a faithful friend.   830
    Longaville. I'll stay with patience; but the time is long.
    Maria. The liker you—few taller are so young.
                              [they talk apart
Berowne. Studies my lady? mistress look on me,
Behold the window of my heart, mine eye,
What humble suit attends thy answer there:
Impose some service on me for thy love.

Rosaline. Oft have I heard of you, my Lord Berowne,
Before I saw you: and the world's large tongue
Proclaims you for a man replete with mocks,
840 Full of comparisons and wounding flouts,
Which you on all estates will execute
That lie within the mercy of your wit.
To weed this wormwood from your fructful brain,
And therewithal to win me, if you please—
Without the which I am not to be won—
You shall this twelvemonth term from day to day
Visit the speechless sick, and still converse
With groaning wretches; and your task shall be,
With all the fierce endeavour of your wit,
850 To enforce the painéd impotent to smile.
    Berowne. To move wild laughter in the throat
        of death?
It cannot be, it is impossible.
Mirth cannot move a soul in agony.
    Rosaline. Why, that's the way to choke a gibing spirit,
Whose influence is begot of that loose grace,
Which shallow laughing hearers give to fools.
A jest's prosperity lies in the ear
Of him that hears it, never in the tongue
Of him that makes it: then if sickly ears,
860 Deafed with the clamours of their own dear groans,
Will hear your idle scorns, continue then,
And I will have you, and that fault withal.
But if they will not, throw away that spirit,
And I shall find you empty of that fault,
Right joyful of your reformation.
    Berowne. A twelvemonth? well; befall what
        will befall,
I'll jest a twelvemonth in an hospital.
            [*the King and the Princess come forward*

Princess. Ay, sweet my lord—and so I take my leave.

King. No madam, we will bring you on your way.

Berowne. Our wooing doth not end like an old play: 870
Jack hath not Jill: these ladies' courtesy
Might well have made our sport a comedy.

King. Come, sir, it wants a twelvemonth an' a day,
And then 'twill end.

Berowne.   That's too long for a play.

ARMADO returns in his proper habit

Armado. Sweet majesty, vouchsafe me,—

Princess. Was not that Hector?

Dumaine. The worthy knight of Troy.

Armado. I will kiss thy royal finger, and take leave.
I am a votary; I have vowed to Jaquenetta
To hold the plough for her sweet love three year.   880
But, most esteemed greatness, will you hear the dialogue
that the two learned men have compiled, in praise of
the owl and the cuckoo? it should have followed in the
end of our show.

King. Call them forth quickly, we will do so.

Armado. Holla! approach.

*An antic draws near: from this side a party of persons
representing Winter, led by one attired as an Owl, and
from that a party representing Spring, led by one attired
as a Cuckoo*

This side is Hiems, winter; this Ver, the spring—the
one maintained by the Owl, th'other by the Cuckoo.
Ver begin.

The Cuckoo sings

890 When daisies pied and violets blue
　　And lady-smocks all silver-white
　And cuckoo-buds of yellow hue
　　Do paint the meadows with delight,
　The cuckoo then on every tree,
　Mocks married men; for thus sings he,
　　　　Cuckoo....
　Cuckoo, cuckoo: O word of fear,
　Unpleasing to a married ear!

　When shepherds pipe on oaten straws,
900　　And merry larks are ploughmen's clocks,
　When turtles tread, and rooks, and daws,
　　And maidens bleach their summer smocks,
　The cuckoo then, on every tree,
　Mocks married men; for thus sings he,
　　　　Cuckoo....
　Cuckoo, cuckoo: O word of fear,
　Unpleasing to a married ear!

The Owl sings

　When icicles hang by the wall,
　　And Dick the shepherd blows his nail,
910　And Tom bears logs into the hall,
　　And milk comes frozen home in pail,
　When blood is nipped, and ways be foul,
　Then nightly sings the staring owl,
　　　　'Tu-who....
　Tu-whit to-who'—a merry note,
　While greasy Joan doth keel the pot.

When all aloud the wind doth blow,
　And coughing drowns the parson's saw,
And birds sit brooding in the snow,
　And Marian's nose looks red and raw,　　920
When roasted crabs hiss in the bowl,
Then nightly sings the staring owl,
　　'Tu-who....
Tu-whit to-who'—a merry note,
　While greasy Joan doth keel the pot.

The words of Mercury are harsh after
the songs of Apollo.

GLOSSARY

GLOSSARY

(Revised in 1960, and indebted to the notes in R. W. David's edition of 1951, and to J. A. K. Thomson's *Shakespeare and the Classics* (1952), pp. 66–77.) *Note*. Where a pun or quibble is intended, the meanings are distinguished as (*a*) and (*b*).

ABATE, omit, except; 5. 2. 541

ABHOMINABLE. A freq. 16th–17th-cent. sp. (explained as < ab homine), inhuman; 5. 1. 24

ABORTIVE, unnatural, unseasonable; 1. 1. 104

ABROGATE SCURRILITY, cut out indecency; 4. 2. 53

ACADEME, a philosophical school or association of students (a not unusual Elizabethan form of 'academy'); 1. 1. 13; 4. 3. 299, 349

ACQUITTANCE, written acknowledgement of a debt; 2. 1. 158

AD UNGUEM, at the fingers' ends (lit. 'to the nail'); 5. 1. 74–7

ADVANCE, raise; 4. 3. 364

ADVISED, (see *well advised*); 5. 2. 434

ADVISED (to be), to take care; 4. 3. 365

AFFECT (sb.), passion, desire; 1. 1, 151

AFFECT (vb.), resort to; 4. 2. 57

AFFECTED, (*a*) in love, (*b*) attacked by disease (see O.E.D. 'affected' III, 1); 2. 1. 230

AFFECTION, (i) love; 4. 3. 286, (ii) affectation; 5. 1. 4

AGATE. Figures were cut in agates for seals (cf. *Ado*, 3. 1. 65); 2. 1. 234

AGONY, the agony of death, the death-throes; 5. 2. 853

AJAX, (i) 'kills sheep' in reference to (*a*) the fights to the death of rams in rut, (*b*) the slaughter of a flock of sheep by Ajax in his madness; 4. 3. 7; (ii) a quibble upon 'a jakes', a stock jest of the age; 5. 2. 575

ALLOWED, permitted the privileges of a fool (cf. *Tw.Nt.* 1. 2. 59; 1. 5. 101); 5. 2. 478

ALLUSION, jest, allegory, riddle (see *exchange*); 4. 2. 42

ALMS-BASKET, a basket in which broken meats from the table of the wealthy were collected for distribution among the poor. Thus 'to live on the alms-basket' = to live upon public charity (O.E.D.); 5. 1. 38

ANTIC, a grotesque pageant, or masque; 5. 1. 109, 142

APPERTINENT TO, belonging to; 1. 2. 16

APOSTROPHUS, usually = the the sign (') indicating the omission of one or more letters, but poss. here = a pedantical word for 'Caesura'; 4. 2. 126

ARGUMENT, (i) proof; 1. 2. 163; (ii) theme; 5. 2. 743

ARGUS, Argus of the hundred eyes was set by Juno as guard over Io to prevent Jupiter making love to her; 3. 1. 198

ARMIPOTENT, mighty in arms (a conventional epithet of Mars; cf. Chaucer, *Knight's Tale*, 1124); 5. 2. 643, 650

ARMS CROSSED, To hold down sorrow (cf. 1. 1. 304; 4. 3. 4–5); 3. 1. 17

ARREST, seize as security; 2. 1. 157

ART, learning, science, magic, the skill or power which learning etc. bestows; 1. 1. 14; 4. 2. 117; 4. 3. 321, 349

ARTERIES, 'the nimble spirits in the arteries', a reference to the old medical notion that the arteries were the channel not only of blood, but also of the vital 'spirits' (q.v.); 4. 3. 302

ARTS-MAN, man of learning or science (see *art*); 5. 1. 77

ASPECT, appearance; 4. 3. 256

ATE, the goddess of mischief and bloodshed; 'more Ates' = more instigation; 5. 2. 686

ATTACH, to seize by the hand; 4. 3. 372

ATTAINDER, 'in a. of' = condemned to; 1. 1 157

BANDY, to strike the ball to and

fro at tennis (cf. 'set of wit'); 5. 2. 29

BARBARISM, ignorance; 1. 1. 112

BARGAIN (sell a), to make a fool of (cf. the modern slang 'sell'); 3. 1. 100, 102

BARK ON TREE (as sure as). The union of bark and tree was commonly taken as the symbol of the married state (see O.E.D. 'bark' 6); 5. 2. 285

BATE, to blunt, with a quibble upon 'bait' = to satisfy the hunger of (cf. 'cormorant devouring Time'); 1. 1. 6

BEADLE, parish constable, who was authorized to whip petty offenders (cf. *John*, 2. 1. 188 'Her injury the beadle to her sin'); 3. 1. 174

BEG, 'You cannot beg us' = You cannot fool us. 'To beg a person' was lit. to petition the court of wards for the custody of a minor, an heiress, or an idiot, as feudal superior (O.E.D.); 5. 2. 490

BEN VENUTO It. 'undertake your b.v.' = ensure your welcome; 4. 2. 164

BESHREW, i.e. may my curse light upon; 5. 2. 46

BETIME, betide; 4. 3. 379

BIAS, natural tendency or leaning. Orig. an oblique or slanting line, but with Sh. it generally refers to the oblique course of a 'wood' at bowls; 4. 2. 116

BIRDBOLT, a blunt wooden-headed heavy arrow, used for shooting small birds from a short distance (cf. *Ado*, 1. 1. 39); 4. 3. 22

BLOOD (in), in full vigour (a hunting phrase); 4. 2. 4

BLOODS, gallant fellows (cf. *John*, 2. 1. 278); 5. 2. 707

BLOW (vb.), (*a*) to blow upon, (*b*) to make to blossom (i.e. blush); 4. 3. 106

BLOW HIS NAILS, see nail; 5. 2. 909

BLUNT, rude, unfeeling; 2. 1. 49

BOARD, (*a*) to board a ship, (*b*) to accost; 2. 1. 216

BODGES, clumsy phrases; 5. 2. 750

BODKIN, a long jewelled pin, with an engraved or modelled top, for ladies' hair. Hart quotes Florio, *New World of Words* (1611), 'a bodkin, a head-needle....also a nice, coy, or selfe-conceited fellow'; 5. 2. 609

BOMBAST, cotton-wool for padding or stuffing; 5. 2. 777

'BONE' FOR 'BENE', see *Laus Deo*, etc.; 5. 1. 27

BOW HAND, see *wide* etc.; 4. 1. 132

BRAWL, 'the most ancient type of figure-dancing' (*Sh. Eng.* II, 446) known in French as the 'branle'; 3. 1. 9

BREAK UP, (*a*) to open a letter (i.e. break the wax), (*b*) to cut up or dismember (a fowl or a deer); 4. 1. 56

BREATHED, in training, with a good wind; 5. 2. 652

BROOCH. An ornament often worn in the hat, Halliwell quoted Taylor, *Wit and Mirth* (1630), 'In Queen Elizabeth's dayes there was a fellow that wore a brooch in his hat like a tooth-drawer with a Rose and Crown and two letters'; 5. 2. 615–17

BROW, (i) countenance; 4. 3. 182, 223; (ii) strike at the b. = strike at the brow-antler, i.e. take good aim. The brow-antler was the lowest part of the stag's horn (see Turberville, *Noble Art of Venerie* (1576), p. 238), and therefore the right mark for the archer; 4. 1. 116.

BUCK, 'A Bucke is called the first yeare a Fawne, the second a Pricket, the third a Sorell, the fourth a Sore, the fifth a Bucke of the first head, and the sixth a Bucke' (Turberville, *Noble Arte of Venerie* (1576), p. 238); 4. 2. 10

BUTT-SHAFT, an unbarbed arrow used in shooting at the butts; 1. 2. 168

CAELUM, Lat. = sky; 4. 2. 5

CALF, dolt, ass; 5. 2. 247–50

CAN, a Northern and archaic form of ''gan', much affected by Spenser and his followers; 4. 3. 103

CANARY (vb.), to move the feet as in the canary, a lively Spanish dance; 3. 1. 12

CANZONET, short song (cf. Thos. Morley, *Canzonets or Little Short Songs to three voyces*, 1593); 4. 2. 127

CAPABLE, (*a*) intelligent, (*b*) of marriageable age; 4. 2. 82

CAPON, (*a*) cock, (*b*) billet-doux (cf. Fr. 'poulet'); 4. 1. 56

CAREER, race or charge in the lists; 5. 2. 482

CARET, Lat. = it is missing; 4. 2. 129

CARRIAGE, demeanour; 5. 2. 306

CARRY, 'it carries it' = it beats everything; 3. 1. 139

CARVE, (a) mod. sense, (b) wave the hand affectedly while speaking (cf. *M.W.W.* 1. 3. 44); 4. 1. 55; 5. 2. 323

CASE, (a) condition, (b) mask (cf. 5. 2. 387); 5. 2. 273

CAUDLE, a warm drink of thin gruel and wine, sweetened and spiced, for sick persons, especially women in child-bed; 4. 3. 171

CAUSE, 'the first and second cause' = lit. reasons according to the laws of the duello for accepting or refusing a challenge; here prob. stands for the laws of the duello in general; 1. 2. 170

CHANGE (a) sc. of the moon, (b) 'a round in dancing' (O.E.D. conj.); 5. 2. 209

CHAPMEN, merchants; 2. 1. 16

CHARGE, i.e. load with arguments, as the cannon is with shot (cf. *mounted*); 5. 2. 88

CHARGE-HOUSE ON THE TOP OF THE MOUNTAIN. Suggests that the 'college' or 'charge-house' kept by Hol. is no better than a sort of Dothe-boys Hall, since it would remind the audience of this well-known passage in Erasmus' *Colloquies*: 'G. Where do you come from? L. From the college of the pointed Mountain [i.e. the Collège de Montaign that Erasmus attended in Paris]. G. Then you come laden with learning? L. No with lice.' [Thomson, pp. 72–3] see also Preface, p. xix; 5. 1. 79

CHIRRAH, Corruption of 'chaere (χαῖρε) hail! [Erasmus; see Thomson, p. 71]; 5. 1. 32

CHUCK, a familiar term of endearment, applied to dear friends and close relatives; 5. 1. 107; 5. 2. 660

CITTERN-HEAD, referring to the grotesquely carved head of the cittern, a common wire-stringed musical instrument of the period; 5. 2. 608

CLAW (vb.), (a) scratch, (b) flatter; 4. 2. 70

CLEAN-TIMBERED, i.e. well-built (Navarre refers sarcastically to Armado's loose, raw-boned figure); 5. 2. 636

CLEAVE, (a) to split or hit (the pin in the centre of the target), (b) to grasp; 4. 1. 136

CLIPT, (a) abbreviated, (b) embraced; 5. 2. 595

CLOSE-STOOL, commode; 5. 2. 574

CLOUD, mask, veil. This is Hart's explanation, and there can be little doubt that he is right (see O.E.D. 'cloud' vb. 3 and cf. 5. 2. 297); 5 2. 204–6

CLOUT, the mark in archery; 4. 1. 133

COCKLE, darnel, tares; 4. 3. 380

COCKLED, with a shell or cockle; 4. 3. 335

CODPIECE, bag-like appendage at the front of a man's hose or breeches; 3. 1. 183

Cog, to cheat (at dice-play); 5. 2. 235

Collusion, 'a trick or ambiguity, in words or reasoning' (O.E.D. 3); 4. 2. 43

Colourable colours, plausible pretexts; 4. 2. 157

Colt, (a) a young horse, (b) a lascivious male (cf. *hackney*); 3. 1. 30

Come upon, attack; 4. 1. 118

Common sense, 'ordinary or untutored perception' (O.E.D.); 1. 1. 57, 64

Comparison, scoffing simile (cf. *Ado*, 2. 1. 154); 5. 2. 840

Competitor, partner; 2. 1. 82

Complement, affectation of courtesy, formal civility ('compliment' is a French word not Englished before the end of the seventeenth cent.); 1. 1. 168, 268; 3. 1. 21; 4. 2. 149

Complete, accomplished, consummate; 1. 1. 136; 1. 2. 44; 3. 1. 11

Complexion, (a) temperament. According to the old medical theory the 'complexion' or composition of man's body was made up of four humours or fluids: blood, phlegm, choler, and melancholy. (b) The colour of the skin; 1. 2. 78–83; 4. 3. 230, 264

Conceit, (i) an ingenious or witty notion; 2. 1. 72; 5. 2. 260; (ii) understanding, wit; 4. 2. 93; 5. 2. 399

Conceited, ingenious; see Q title-page, p. 1

Concolinel, obscure, probably corrupt. Presumably = title

or opening words of the song; 3. 1. 3

Condign, well-merited (archaic in a 'good' sense, but so used by Spenser); 1. 2. 25

Confounded, ruined, destroyed; 5. 2. 517

Congruent, fitting, agreeable (an affected word, not found elsewhere in Shakespeare); 1. 2. 13; 5. 1. 89

Consonant, nonentity (a consonant not being able to stand by itself like a vowel); 5. 1. 50

Continent, total, sum; 4. 1. 109

Continent canon, variously explained as (a) the law enjoining continence, (b) the law contained in the edict; Armado probably means both; 1. 1. 254

Copper, ? false coin. Perhaps a ref. to the copper farthings issued in 1594, the earliest of English copper coins (see *Sh. Eng.* 1, 344); 4. 3. 383

Cormorant, gluttonous; 1. 1. 4

Corner-cap, 'a cap with four (or three) corners, worn by divines and members of the universities in 16–17th c.' (O.E.D.). No one has yet noticed that it was also worn by judges (and still is, when passing sentence of death) but the whole context shows that Berowne has this use in mind (see Renton, *Encyc. Laws of Eng.*: 'black cap'). It must also be noted that the ecclesiastical corner-cap was being hotly attacked by the

CORNER-CAP (*cont.*)
Puritans at this period.
Stubbes (*Anatomy of Abuses*,
1583, pt. II, ed. Furnivall,
p. 115) writes: 'The cor-
nered cappe, say these mis-
terious fellows [the Papists]
doth signifie, and represent
the whole monarchy of the
world, East, West, North
and South, the gouernment
whereof standeth vpon them,
as the cappe doth vppon their
heades.' Here is Berowne's
'corner-cap of society'. To
the Elizabethans the corner-
cap symbolized authority
(cf. *Tyburn*); 4. 3. 51

CORPORALL, champion; 'corporal of the field' = 'a superior officer of the army in
the 16th and 17th cent.,
who acted as an assistant or
a kind of aide-de-camp to
the sergeant-major (= the
modern "adjutant")"
(O.E.D.). It is to be noted
that there were *four* of these
officers in each regiment;
3. 1. 186; 4. 3. 83

COSTARD, lit. a large kind of
apple, but commonly applied
(orig. humorously) to the
head; 3. 1. 69

COUPLEMENT, couple. A Spen-
serian word (cf. *F.Q.* VI, v.
24 'And forth together rode,
a comely couplement'); 5. 2.
529

CRAB, crab-apple; 5. 2. 921

CRACK, boast of; 4. 3. 264

CRITIC, fault-finder, jeerer; 3.
1. 175; 4. 3. 167

CROSSES, coins (with crosses
stamped upon them)—a

common jest of the period;
1. 2. 33

CUCKOO-BUDS, unexplained; the
marsh marigold, the butter-
cup and the cowslip have all
been suggested; 5. 2. 892

CURIOUS-KNOTTED, i.e. quaintly
designed or laid out. A knot
= a laid-out flower-bed (see
Sh. Eng. I, 371, 377); 1. 1.
243

CURST, shrewish; 4. 1. 36

CURTSY, bow (of any kin
1. 2. 62

DAMASK, the colour of the
damask rose, i.e. a blush-
colour (cf. *A.Y.L.* 3. 5.
120—3 'a pretty redness....
just the difference between
the constant red and min-
gled damask'); 5. 2. 296

DANCING-HORSE, Banks's well-
known performing horse,
Morocco; 1. 2. 53

DAZZLING (intrans.) becoming
dim or dazzled (cf. *V.A.*
1064, 3 *Hen. VI*, 2. 1. 25);
1. 1. 82

DEAR, grievous, dire; 5. 2. 787,
860

DEAREST, best, 2. 1. 1.

DEAREST SPIRIT, best wit; 2.
1. 1

DEATH, 'to the d.' = if we die
for it; 5. 2. 146

DEATH'S FACE, a skull.
'Death's-head rings with
the motto, memento mori,
were very popular' (Hart);
5. 2. 610

DEBATE, contention. A Spen-
serian word (*F.Q.* II, viii, 54
'the whole debate'); 1. 1.
173

DEGREE, rank; 5. 2. 505

DENY, refuse; 5. 2. 228, 703, 807, 809

DEPART WITHAL, part with, surrender; 2. 1. 144

DEUCE-ACE, a low throw at dice, a two and a one. In the game of 'hazard', which is here referred to, if the player threw two aces (= ames-ace, see *All's Well*, 2. 3. 85) or a deuce-ace, he lost the game (see *Sh. Eng.* II, 470); 1. 2. 46

DEY-WOMAN, dairy-woman; 1. 2. 126

DICK, fellow. A term of contempt; 5. 2. 464

DICTYNNA, a recondite name for the moon. Steevens suggests that Sh. may have found this unusual title for Diana in the second book of Golding's translation of Ovid's *Metamorphoses*: 'Dictynna garded with her traine and proud of killing deere'; 4. 2. 36

DIGNITY, (a) worth, (b) grandeur; 4. 3. 232

DIGRESSION, transgression; 1. 2. 113

DISPOSED, in a jocund mood, inclined to mirth (cf. *Tw. Nt.* 2. 3. 88); 2. 1. 248; 5. 2. 466

DOMINICAL, the red letter (? with a gold background), denoting the Sundays (dies dominica) in the old almanacs. Rosaline is of course glancing at Katherine's amber (4. 3. 84) hair, which might be called either 'golden' or 'red'; 5. 2. 44

DOTER, fond lover; 4. 3. 257

DOUBLE TONGUE, (a) deceitful tongue, (b) alluding to the leather tongue on the inside of a mask held in the mouth to keep it in place; 5. 2. 245

DRY, dull, stupid (cf. *Tw.Nt.* 1. 3. 81; 1. 5. 44); 5. 2. 373

DRY-BEATEN, severely beaten (cf. *Errors*, G. 'dry'); 5. 2. 263

DUELLO, the art of duelling, its code and practice. O.E.D. quotes no earlier use of the word than this, and Sh.'s references to the new-fangled duelling with the rapier are uniformly contemptuous (see *cause, passado*, and *M.W.W.* G. 'fencing'); 1. 2. 172

DUTY, i.e. curtsy; 4. 2. 150

EAGLE-SIGHTED, i.e. able to gaze upon the sun (cf. 4. 3. 330–1); 4. 3. 222

ENTER, entry. Theat. term; 5. 1. 130

ENVIOUS, spiteful; 1. 1. 100

EPITHET, Nathaniel means 'synonym'; 4. 2. 8

EPITHETON, descriptive term; orig. form of 'epithet'; 1. 2. 14

ESTATES, classes, ranks; 'on all estates' = on all sorts of persons without discrimination; 5. 2. 841

EXCHANGE, 'th'allusion holds in the exchange = either (i) 'the jest lies in the change of the moon' (Brae), 'exchange' being a pedantic word for 'change', or (ii) 'the riddle is as good when I

EXCHANGE (*cont.*)
use the name of Adam as when you use the name of Cain' (Warburton); 4. 2. 42

EXCREMENT, any outgrowth of the body, e.g. hair, nails; 5. 1. 101

EXHALE, draw forth; 4. 3. 68

EXPLICATION, explanation; Hol.'s word; 4. 2. 14

EXTEMPORAL, extempore; 1. 2. 175; 4. 2. 50

FACILITY, fluency; 4. 2. 129

FADGE, serve, fit, be suitable; 5. 1. 142

FAIR FALL! good luck to!; 2. 1. 121

FAIRING, lit. a present bought at a fair; hence, a complimentary gift of any kind; 5. 2. 2

FALCHION, sword; 5. 2. 613

FALSELY, treacherously; 1. 1. 76

FAMILIAR, (i) familiar spirit; 1. 2. 165; (ii) intimate friend; 5. 1. 93

FANATICAL, frantic, extravagant; 5. 1. 18

FARBOROUGH, mispronunciation of 'Tharborough', i.e. thirdborough, a petty constable; 1. 1. 184

FAST AND LOOSE, an old cheating game (associated with gypsies); 1. 2. 150; 3. 1. 102

FAT, slow-witted, dull; 5. 2. 268

FAUSTE, PRECOR, etc. 'I pray thee, Faustus, while all our cattle ruminate in the cool shade.' The opening words of the first eclogue of Mantuan (q.v.). The quotation

is not inappropriate to the sylvan surroundings; 4. 2. 99–100

FESTINATELY, quickly (a pedantic word); 3. 1. 6

FIERCE, ardent, eager; 5. 2. 849

FILED, polished; 5. 1. 10

FIRE-NEW, brand-new; 1. 1. 178

FIREWORK, pyrotechnic display (very popular at this period); 5. 1. 109

FIRST AND SECOND CAUSE, technical excuses to escape a duel (cf. *A.Y.L.* 5. 4. 66 ff.); 1. 2. 170

FLAP-DRAGON, a burning raisin or plum floating alight in liquor and swallowed by topers. The term in contemporary allusion generally has reference to swaggering. Cost. is hitting at the braggart; 5. 1. 42

FLASK, 'carved-bone face on a flask', alluding to the carved ornament on a soldier's powder-horn; 5. 2. 614

FLATTER UP, pamper, coddle; 5. 2. 810

FLATTERY, charm, palliation (cf. O.E.D. 'flatter' vb. 3, 6); 4. 3. 282

FLEERED, grinned; 5. 2. 109

FLOURISH, varnish, embellishment; 2. 1. 14; 4. 3. 234

FOOL, 'used as a term of endearment or pity' (O.E.D.); 2. 1. 182; 4. 3. 78

FORCE, to attach importance to (cf. *Lucr.* 1021 'I force not argument a straw'); 5. 2. 440

FORFEIT, see *Sue*; 5 2. 425–7

FORM, (a) order, orderly performance, (b) excellence, proficiency (see O.E.D. 'form' 6); 5. 2. 517

FORTUNA DE LA GUERRA, the fortune of war; 5. 2. 528

FREE, (a) untainted by disease, (b) unattached to a lover; 5. 2. 424

FRENCH CROWN, (a) the 'écu', a French gold coin, (b) the baldness produced by the 'French disease', i.e. syphilis; 3. 1. 140

FRIEND, sweetheart; 5. 2. 404

GALL, (a) a raw or sore place, (b) bile, bitterness of spirit; 'thou grievest my gall' = you annoy me; 5. 2. 237

GALLOWS (adj.), i.e. gallows-bird, one who deserves hanging; 5. 2. 12

GEAR, dress; 5. 2. 306

GELDED, mutilated, depreciated in value (of landed property); 2. 1. 146

GENEROUS, (Lat. generosus) noble, high-born; 5. 1. 88

GENTILITY, politeness, good manners; 1. 1. 128

GENTLE, lit. well-born: hence, gracious, kind; 4. 3. 234

GERMAN CLOCK, 'one of elaborate construction, often containing automatic figures of persons or animals' (O.E.D.). Such clocks were very liable to get out of order; 3. 1. 189

GIG, a whipping-top; 4. 3. 164; 5. 1. 63, 65

GILT, 'a gilt nutmeg', i.e. 'endored', or glazed with the yoke of an egg (cf. the proverbial 'gilded pill'). Gilt nutmegs, for spicing ale or wine, were a common lover's gift at this time (Hart); 5. 2. 645

GIVE HORNS, i.e. make a husband a cuckold; 5. 2. 252

GLOZES, pretences, disguises, 'high-falutin talk' (Onions); 4. 3. 367

GNAT, i.e. an insignificant creature that flutters about a light; 4. 3. 163

GOD-DIG-YOU-DEN, i.e. God give you good even; 4. 1. 42

GOD'S BLESSING ON YOUR BEARD! may you have sense more fitting a grey beard!; 2. 1. 201

GOLDEN LETTER (see dominical); 5. 2. 44

GOOD WORD, kindness; 4. 2. 91; 5. 2. 274

GO TO! Come! come! 3. 1. 200

GREASILY, indecently, smuttily; 4. 1. 136

GREEN GOOSE, a young goose (lit. a goose hatched in the autumn, green-fed in spring and sold in May). It seems clear from the contexts that Berowne means what would now be vulgarly called 'a flapper' (lit. = a young duck); 1. 1. 97; 4. 3. 73

GROSS (by), wholesale; 5. 2. 319

GROUND, basis, fundamental principle, the elements or rudiments of a study; 4. 3. 269, 299

GUARDS, ornamental borders or trimmings; 4. 3. 56

HA?, eh? 3. 1. 52

HACKNEY, (a) a horse kept for hire, (b) prostitute; 3. 1. 31

HALF, 'your half '—your wife; 5. 2. 249

HALF-CHEEK, profile; 5. 2. 615

HALFPENNY PURSE, a minute purse, halfpennies being tiny silver coins at this period (cf. *M.W.W.* 3. 5. 133); 5. 1. 70

HANDS (of all), in any case, whatever happens; 4. 3. 215

HAUD CREDO, Lat. = I do not believe it; Dull supposes 'credo' to be a kind of 'doe'; 4. 2. 11 ff.

HAUNTED, frequented; 1. 1. 162

HAVE AT YOU! Here's for you! 4. 3. 286

HAVE TO DO WITH, 'to have dealings or business with; to have connexion or intercourse (of any kind) with' (O.E.D. 'do' 33. 9); 5. 2. 428

HAY, 'a country dance having a winding or serpentine movement, or being of the nature of a reel' (O.E.D.); 5. 1. 149

HEAR, 'do you hear?'—listen!; 2. 1. 255

HEAVY, stupid with grief; 5. 2. 14

HEDGE-PRIEST, unlearned priest in minor orders; 5. 2. 539

HEED, that which one heeds or attends to (a rare meaning of the word); 1. 1. 82; 'suspicious watch' (Schmidt); 4. 3. 333

HIGHT, is called (deliberately archaic); 1. 1. 170

HIND, (a) stag, (b) peasant 1 2. 115

HIT IT, cf. *Wily Beguiled* (pub. 1606), Mal. Soc. Reprint, ll. 2451–7 'Thou art my Ciperlillie: | And I thy Trangdidowne dilly, | And sing hey ding a ding ding: | And do the tother thing, | And when tis done not misse, | To giue my wench a kisse: | And then dance canst thou not hit it?' and *The Wit of a Woman* (pub. 1604), Mal. Soc. Reprint, ll. 174–9 'You are Sir Nimbleheeles, and you shall bee a dauncing-maister to teach the wenches to daunce; so when you haue your mistresse, hange your selfe, if you can not teach her a right hit it, both in time and place to iumpe euen with the instrument.' We owe the second quotation to Prof. Moore Smith; 4. 1. 120, 123–5.

HOBBY-HORSE, (a) a figure in the morris-dance, 'formed by a man inside a frame fitted with the head and tail of a horse, and with trappings reaching to the ground and hiding the feet of the actor, who pranced and curvetted about' (*Sh. Eng.* II, 438). 'The hobby-horse is forgot', which recurs in *Ham.* 3. 2. 146 and constantly elsewhere in Eliz. literature, is generally supposed to be a quotation from some ballad satirizing the Puritan opposition to

Hobby-horse (*cont.*)
morris-dancing; but this is pure supposition, and it is not clear whether 'forgot' meant 'omitted' or 'out-of-fashion'; (*b*) a prostitute; 3. 1. 28–30.

Honorificabilitudinitatibus, a jest of the medieval schools, supposed to be the longest word known. The nominative is a real word, and means 'the state of being loaded with honours'; 5. 1. 41

Horn-book, a spelling primer, 'framed in wood and covered with a thin plate of transparent horn'; on this piece of paper the consonants were generally given first, next the vowels, each surmounted by a horizontal stroke or horn, and, after these, simple combinations of vowels and consonants, such as *ab, eb, ib, ba, be, bi,* etc., followed by the Lord's Prayer and so on (see *Sh. Eng.* 1, 228, illustration); 5. 1. 45

House-keeping, hospitality; 2. 1. 103

How? Well, what about it? 5. 2. 598

Humble, kind, civil; 5. 2. 627

Humility, humanity (cf. *M.V.* G.); 4. 3. 346

Humorous, moody, fanciful; 3. 1. 174

Humour (vb.), adapt oneself to; 3. 1. 12

Illustrate, illustrious; 4. 1. 64; 5. 1. 117

Imitari, Lat. = to copy; 4. 2. 132

Imp, lit. sapling, scion (without any necessary connexion with evil); hence, youngster; 1. 2. 5; 5. 2. 584

In, involved; 4. 3. 18

Incision, blood-letting; 4. 3. 94

Inconsiderate, thoughtless, brainless; 3. 1. 77

Incony, delicious, rare, fine, pretty, 'a cant word of uncertain origin' (O.E.D.); 3. 1. 134; 4. 1. 141

Indiscreet, unwise; 4. 2. 29

Infamonize, defame (Arm.'s speech); 5. 2. 677

Inherit, possess, own; 1. 1. 73; 4. 1. 20

Inheritor, owner; 2. 1. 5

Inkle, a kind of linen tape; 3. 1. 138

Insania, madness; 5. 1. 25

Insinuateth me of, lit. inserts (madness) into me; 5. 1. 24

Insinuation, insertion; Hol.'s word; 4. 2. 14

Intellect, Probably a far-fetched pun: 'understanding' > subscript; 4. 2. 139

Intelligisne, Domine? Lat. = do you understand, sir?' 5. 1. 25

Interim, something done during an interval, respite; 1. 1. 171

Intimation, Gen. glossed suggestion, but Hol. probably means 'interruption' (< late Lat. 'intimare' = to thrust into (see Thomson, p. 68); 4. 2. 13

Inward, secret, privy; 5. 1. 94

JERKS OF INVENTION, sallies of
wit. 'A very proper figure
for a schoolmaster's use,
since "jerking" was equi-
valent to whipping' (Hart);
4. 2. 132

JEW, unexplained. It recurs in
M.N.D. 3. 1. 97 'Most
brisky Juvenal, and eke
most lovely Jew', but is not
found elsewhere. The
M.N.D. parallel suggests
that it is simply a playful
diminutive of 'Juvenal'
(q.v.); 3. 1. 134

JIG (sb.), a rapid lively dance-
tune; 4. 3. 165

JIG (vb.), to sing or play as a
jig; 3. 1. 11

JOAN, a generic name for a
country wench; 3. 1. 204;
4. 3. 179; 5. 2. 916, 925

JUVENAL. If Moth be a carica-
ture upon Nashe, as is possible, this epithet was intended to recall Greene's
phrase 'young Iuuenall, that
byting Satyrist' (*Groats-
worth of Wit*, 1592). But
'juvenal' came to be used by
the Eliz. as equivalent to
'juvenile' (cf. *M.N.D.* 3. 1.
97, 2 *Hen. IV*, 1. 2. 22,
Mere's *Wit's Treasurie*,
1598, 'gallant young Iuuenall', etc.); 1. 2. 8; 3. 1. 65

KEEL, 'to cool a hot or boiling
liquid, by stirring, skimming,
or pouring in something
cold, in order to prevent it
from boiling over' (O.E.D.);
5. 2. 916, 925

KEEP, inhabit, keep to; 4. 3.
321

8

KILL THE HEART, utterly dis-
courage; 5. 2. 149

LADY-SMOCK, generally in-
terpreted 'cuckoo-flower',
which, however, is pale
lilac, not 'silver-white'; we
suggest 'stitchwort', the
whitest of all spring flowers;
5. 2. 891

LADY WALLED ABOUT WITH
DIAMONDS, a piece of jewel-
lery much affected at this
time, in the form either of a
brooch or a pendant; the
figure might be a nude (presumably allegorical) or a
portrait of some living person (cf. *Sh. Eng.* II, 114–15);
5. 2. 3

LAND, possibly = 'laund', i.e.
a glade; 5. 2. 309

LARGE, loose, liberal, copious;
5. 2. 838

LAUS DEO, BONE, INTELLIGO,
God be praised, my good
friend, I understand. But
Hol. takes 'bone' to be an
error for 'bene' (Schmidt);
5. 1. 27

LEADEN SWORD, imitation sword
(a stage property); 5. 2. 481

LEGE, DOMINE, Lat. = read,
sir; 4. 2. 110–11

LEMON STUCK WITH CLOVES,
App. for spicing ale; 5. 2.
646–7

L'ENVOY, the short stanza at
the conclusion of a poem,
often defining the point of
the poem, e.g. as in Sh.'s
sonnets; 3. 1. 70–103

LIABLE, apt; 5. 1. 89

LIBBARD, properly, a leopard;
but 'libbard' and 'lion' were

LIBBARD (*cont.*)
synonymous terms in respect of the English royal coat of arms (see O.E.D. 'leopard' 2 *b*); 5. 2. 545

LIBERAL, too free, (almost) indecorous; 5. 2. 729

LIE, lodge, sojourn; 1. 1. 148

LIGHT, loose; 1. 2. 119; 2. 1. 197; 5. 2. 15, 20

LIKELIEST; 4. 2. 91

LION THAT HOLDS HIS POLL-AXE, the traditional representation of Alexander's arms; 5. 2. 573

LIVER, formerly considered the seat of the passions; 4. 3. 72

LOFTY, sublime, (or poss.) haughty; 5. 1. 10

'LONG OF, along of, owing to; 2. 1. 117

LOOSE (sb.), 'at his very loose' = at the very last moment (an archery term); 5. 2. 738

LOOSE (adj.), random, not serious, with a quibble upon 'loose-fitting'; 5. 2. 762

LORD HAVE MERCY ON US, written upon the door of a plague-stricken house; 5. 2. 419

LORD'S TOKENS (the), marks or spots which appeared on the patient at the last stage of the plague; here a quibble; 5. 2. 423

LOVE, appraise, set a value upon (see O.E.D. vb.² 2). Berowne means that through love alone men have value; 4. 3. 355

LOW-SPIRITED, base; 1. 1. 244

LUSTRE, gleam; 4. 2. 92

MAGNIFICENT, vainglorious, arrogant; the obvious meaning at 3. 1. 177, and the secondary, if not the primary, meaning at 1. 1. 191

MAIL, wallet, budget; 3. 1. 72

MAINTAIN, defend; 5. 2. 888

MALMSEY, a strong sweet wine; 5. 2. 233

MANAGE, 'a short gallop at full speed' in a riding-school (O.E.D.); 5. 2. 482

MANAGER, wielder, controller; 1. 2. 174

MANNER (taken with the), more properly, 'taken with the mainour', i.e. in the act; 1. 1. 202

MANTUAN, i.e. Battista Spagnuoli of Mantua (d. 1516), whose *Eclogues* became a school text-book all over Europe; 4. 2. 100

Manu cita, with swift hand; 5. 1. 65

MARGENT, margin of a page, the commentary or illuminated border in such a margin; 2. 1. 244 (where Boyet means the eyes, which are the 'illumination' of the face); 5. 2. 8

MARK, target, butt, anything at which aim is taken; 4. 1. 129

MARKET (ended the), an allusion to the proverb 'three women and a goose make a market'; 3. 1. 109

MEAN, the tenor part; 5. 2. 328

MEASURABLE, meet, competent; 5. 1. 89

MEASURE, a stately dance; 5. 2. 185

MEHERCLE! by Hercules! 4. 2. 83

MERIT, (a) payment for service done, (b) (theol.) works;
4. 1. 21

MESS, lit. a party of four seated at one table and feeding from the same dish; 4. 3. 203;
5. 2. 361

METE AT, aim at; 4. 1. 131

METHEGLIN, a variety of mead, spiced with herbs; 5. 2. 233

MINIME, by no means; 3. 1. 59

MINSTRELSY, domestic or court entertainers. Not necessarily musicians; 1. 1. 176

MISPRISION, misapprehension; 4. 3. 95

MISTAKEN, MISTOOK, miscarried, taken to the wrong person; 4. 1. 57, 105

MONARCHO, a crazy Italian who haunted Elizabeth's court some time before 1580, at which date Churchyard published a poem entitled *The Phantastical Monarkes Epitaphe*. From this, and from other contemporary references, it appears that the man was a harmless madman, suffering from megalomania; his 'climyng mynde', says Churchyard, 'aspierd beyonde the starrs'; 4. 1. 98

MOONSHINE IN THE WATER, appearance without reality, foolishness just moonshine; 5. 2. 208

MORTIFIED, dead to the pleasures of the world (a theological expression); 1. 1. 28

MOTION, sc. of body or mind (cf. *Caes.* G.); 5. 2. 216–17

MOUNTED, set up in position (like a gun); 5. 2. 82

MOUSE, a playful term of endearment; 5. 2. 19

MUCH UPON THIS, 'TIS = That's about the size of it; 5. 2. 472

MUTTON AND PORRIDGE, i.e. mutton-broth (with perhaps a side-glance at 'mutton' = a loose woman); 1. 1. 292–3

NAIL (blow one's), to wait patiently while one has nothing to do (Hart), not 'warm one's hands', as it has been generally interpreted;
5. 2. 909

NATIVE, by nature; 1. 2. 103

NICE, modest, shy, fastidious, refined; 3. 1. 22; 5. 2. 219, 222, 232, 325

NICKNAME (vb.), to call by an incorrect or improper name (cf. *Ham.* 3. 1. 151 'you nickname God's creatures');
5. 2. 349

NINE WORTHIES, traditionally these were Hector, Alexander, Julius Caesar, Joshua, David, Judas Maccabaeus, Arthur, Charlemagne, and Guy of Warwick or Godfrey of Bouillon. The list varies with different writers but Hercules and Pompey are not found elsewhere;
5. 1. 113

NIT, lit. the egg of a louse; hence, a very small insect or fly; 4. 1. 147

NO POINT, a phrase from the French = not at all (with a quibble upon 'the point of a knife or sword'); 2. 1. 188;
5. 2. 277

NORTH POLE, the pole star, symbol of constant determination, 'the ever fixéd pole' (*Oth.* 2. 1. 15); 5. 2. 691

NOTE, stigma, brand; 4. 3. 122; 5. 2. 75

NOVI HOMINEM TANQUAM TE, I know the man as well as I know you. A phrase from Lyly's *Grammar*; 5. 1. 9

NOVUM, a dice-game properly called 'novem quinque' from its two principal throws, nine and five. Berowne is referring to the presentation of nine worthies by five players; 5. 2. 541

NUMBERS RATIFIED, metrically correct verse; 4. 2. 128

O, a small circle or spot (Rosaline means 'pock mark'). Cf. *M.N.D.* 3. 2. 188 (star), *Hen. V*, 1st chor. 13 (the Globe theatre), *Ant.* 5. 2. 81 (the earth), and Cotgrave, 1611 (a spangle on a dress); 5. 2. 45

OBSCENELY, Costard, like Bottom (*M.N.D.* 1. 2. 111) appears to think that the word is connected with 'seen' and means 'openly, clearly, so as to be seen'; 4. 1. 142

ODE, ditty—applied to lyrical verse in general at this period; 4. 3. 96

O LORD, SIR, a common exclamation = surely, certainly (cf. *All's Well* 2. 2.); 1. 2 6; 5. 2. 485

OMNE BENE, Lat. = all is well; 4. 2. 30

OPINION, self-conceit; 5. 1. 5

OSTENTATION, (i) show. Arm., as usual, strains the sense a little and makes it = spectacle; 5. 1. 108; (ii) vanity, pretension; 5. 2. 409

OUT O'TH' WAY, beside the point, gone astray; 4. 3. 74

OUTSWEAR, forswear (cf. *swear out*); 1. 2. 63

O'ERPARTED, having too difficult a part, or too many parts to play; 5. 2. 581

O'ERSHOT, wide of the mark; 4. 3. 157

OWE, own; 1. 2. 103; 2. 1. 6

OX, 'to make an ox of one = to make one a fool (cf. *M.W.W.* 5. 5. 116); 5. 2. 250

PAIN, (*a*) toil, (*b*) penalty; 1. 1. 73

PAINFUL, paintstaking; 2. 1. 23

PAINTED, feigning, specious; 2. 1. 14; 4. 3. 235

PAINTED CLOTH, cloth or canvas, used as hangings for the wall or for partitions in a room, and painted in oil. 'The Worthies' was a favourite subject for such paintings at this period (cf. 'scraped out'); 5. 2. 573

PARFECT, Costard's blunder for 'perform'; 5. 2. 501

PARITOR, 'an apparitor or paritor is the officer of the bishop's court who carries out citations: as citations are most frequently issued for fornication, the paritor is put under Cupid's government' (Johnson); 3. 1. 185

PARTI-COATED, in motley; 5. 2. 762

Pass, to accomplish, execute, enact (cf. O.E.D. 'pass' 45 and *Shrew*, 4. 4. 57 'We'll pass the business privately and well'); 5. 1. 124

Passado, from the Spanish 'passada' = a forward thrust with the sword, one foot being advanced at the same time (*Sh. Eng.* ii, 398); 1. 2. 171

Passion (vb.), to be affected with passion or deep feeling (cf. Spenser, *F.Q.* ii, ix, 41); 1. 1. 255

Patch, fool. 'So were there a patch set on learning' = so a fool would be set on to learn; 4. 2. 31

Pathetical, moving (not solely to pity, as in the mod. sense); 1. 2. 95; 4. 1. 147

Pauca verba, few words— almost = not a word! 4. 2. 171

Pavilion, tent for a champion at a tournament; 5. 2. 653

Peal, a salvo of ordnance (O.E.D. sb. 5.) Armado is about to fire off; 5. 1. 43

Pell-mell, lit. 'confusedly, without keeping ranks', and so 'headlong, recklessly'; 4. 3. 365

Penance, possibly blunder for 'pleasure' (R.W.D.); 1. 2. 124

Pencil, a paint-brush for a lady's toilet; 5. 2. 43

Pennyworth, bargain; 3. 1. 101

Pepin (King), first of the Carlovingian kings, died A.D. 768; representative, therefore, of hoary antiquity; 4. 1. 119

Peregrinate, foreign fashioned. This 'singular and choice epithet' may be intended to suggest the astrological term 'peregrine' used of a planet out of its appropriate position in the zodiac; 5. 1. 14

Peremptory, arrogant, overbearing, dictatorial; 4. 3. 222; 5. 1. 10

Perge, Lat. = proceed; 4. 2. 53

Perjure, perjurer. Perjurers at this period were punished by being publicly exhibited with a paper on head or breast, setting forth their guilt (cf. 'from my forehead wipe a perjured note', 4. 3. 122); 4. 3. 45

Phantasime, fantastic being (not found elsewhere, cf. *Monarcho*); 4. 1. 98; 5. 1. 18

Physic, physician; 2. 1. 186

Pia mater, brain (lit. a membrane enclosing the brain); 4. 2. 76

Pick, with a quibble upon 'pick' = throw, cast; 5. 2. 542

Picked, fastidious; 5. 1. 13

Pin (sb.), 'a peg, nail or stud fixed in the centre of a target' (O.E.D. cf. *Rom.* 2. 4. 15); 4. 1. 135

Pin (vb.), 'pins the wenches on his sleeve' = i.e. flaunt their dependance upon him (see O.E.D. 'pin' 4) 5. 2. 321

Pitch a toil, set a snare; 4. 3. 3

Placket, petticoat, or a slit in same; 3. 1. 183

Plantain, the application of a plantain-leaf as the popular remedy for bruises and wounds is constantly re-

ferred to in Eliz. literature;
3. 1. 72

PLANTED, set up, furnished.
The word was specially connected at this time with the
establishment, or 'planta-
tion', of new colonies; 1. 1.
164

PLEA, that which is claimed (a
rare use, but cf. *M. of V.* 3.
2. 285; 4. 1. 198, 203); 2. 1. 7

PLEASANT, merry, facetious;
4. 1. 128

PLEASE-MAN, ? (a coined word),
'officious parasite' (Charl-
ton); 5. 2. 463

POINT (vb.), direct; 2. 1. 243

POINT-DEVISE, extremely precise, perfectly correct; 5. 1. 18

POLE, probably the long staff
used by thieves on the
Border (see David, note *ad
hoc*); 5. 2. 692

POMEWATER, a large juicy kind
of apple, popular in the six-
teenth cent. but now for-
gotten; 4. 2. 4

POMPION, a pumpkin (often
'applied in contempt to a big
man' O.E.D. 3, cf. 'his
great limb or joint', 5. 1.
124); 5. 2. 502

PORRIDGE, broth; 1. 1. 293

POST, ride as quickly as possible; 4. 3. 185

PREAMBULATE, go on before;
5. 1. 77

PREPOSTEROUS, highly improper, quite out of place (Arm.
writes affectedly); 1. 1. 239

PRETTY AND, pretty (adv.)
quite, very (see O.E.D. 5, c);
1. 2. 18

PREYFUL, killing much prey;
4. 2. 56

PRICK (sb.), the spot in the
centre of a target, the bull's
eye (for the quibble, cf. *Rom.*
2. 4. 119); 2. 1. 187; 4. 1.
131, 137

PRICKET, see *buck*; 4. 2. 12, 21,
49, 52, 58

PRINT (in), precisely; 3. 1. 170

PRISCIAN, a late Lat. gram-
marian, fl. A.D. 525; 5. 1. 28

PROMETHEAN FIRE, the fire of
heaven, such as Prometheus
stole, acc. to Greek mytho-
logy; 4. 3. 300, 348

PROTESTATION, solemn dec-
laration; 1. 1. 33

PROUD, sensually excited (cf.
Lucr. 712, *Two Gent.* G.
'proud', *Errors*, G. 'pride');
5. 2. 66

PRUNE, dress up, trim; 4. 3. 180

PURGATION, (*a*) laxative, (*b*)
cleansing from guilt or sus-
picion; 3. 1. 125

PURSENT, Costard's form of
present, i.e. represent; 5. 2.
488

PUSH-PIN, 'a child's game in
which each player pushes or
fillips his pin with the object
of crossing that of another
player' (O.E.D.); 4. 3. 166

PUT OFF, baffle, repulse; 4. 1.
109

PUT ON, Schmidt explains 'lay
on, as a blow'; 4. 1. 112

QUALM, a sudden feeling of
faintness, or of sickness (with
a quibble upon 'calm', cf.
2 Hen IV, 2. 4. 40); 5. 2.
279

QUICK RECREATION, 'lively
sport, spritely diversion'
(Johnson); 1. 1. 161

QUILLET, subtlety, evasive shift verbal nicety; 4. 3. 284

QUONDAM, former; 5. 1. 6

QUOTE, (i) to refer to by citing the page or chapter of a book; 2. 1. 244; (ii) to regard or set down as being so and so (cf. *All's Well*, 5. 3. 205 'He's quoted for a most perfidious slave'); 4. 3. 84; 5. 2. 782

QUOTH, say; 4. 3. 106, 217

RACKED, tortured, examined under torture; 5. 2. 814

RAGE, madness; 5. 2. 417

RATIFY, lit. = make correctly; 4. 2. 128

RATIONAL HIND, intelligent rustic; 1. 2. 115

RAUGHT, reached; 4. 2. 41

RECKONING, keeping accounts; 1. 2. 40; 5. 2. 497

RED DOMINICAL, see *dominical*; 5. 2. 44

REPREHEND, blunder for 'apprehend' by confusion with 'represent'; 1. 1. 183

RESOLVE ME, give me a decision; 2. 1. 109

RIDICULOUS, giving rise to laughter (Armado's speech); 3. 1. 76

RIGHT, straight; 5. 2. 562

RUBBING, 'The Rub is any obstacle or impediment which diverts the bowl from its course. It is a feature that lends itself to punning and metaphorical application' (*Sh. Eng.* II, 464; cf. *Troil.* 3. 2. 50 'So, so; rub on, and kiss the mistress'); 4. 1. 138

RUB THE ELBOW, cf. mod. 'rub one's hands' to express pleasurable satisfaction or glee; 5. 2. 109

SALVE, (*a*) ointment, (*b*) the salutation; 3. 1. 71, 77, 78

SANS, (< Fr.) without. In common use but regarded as affected; 5. 2. 415

SATIS QUOD SUFFICIT, i.e. enough is as good as a feast; 5. 1. 1

SAUCY, insolent, presumptuous; 1. 1. 85

SAW, discourse; 5. 2. 918

SCHOOL OF NIGHT, if text not corrupt, probably denotes a coterie of the day to which Raleigh, Harriot, and Chapman belonged, which dabbled in astronomy and held unorthodox religious opinions; 4. 3. 251

SEA-WATER GREEN, colour associated with courtesy (cf. Linthicum, p. 31); 1. 2. 82

SELF, the same; 4. 1. 36

SENSE OF SENSE (the), the apprehension of the senses; 5. 2. 258

SENSIBLE, (i) sensitive; 4. 3. 334; (ii) effective, striking; 5. 2. 259

SENSIBLY, (*a*) as mod. (*b*) with emotion; 3. 1. 112

SERVE ONE'S TURN, (*a*) be of service to, (*b*) satisfy sexually; 1. 1. 288–9

SEVERAL, 'Several is an enclosed field of a private proprietor; so Katharine says, her lips are private property. Of a lord that was newly married one observed that he grew fat; Yes, said Sir Walter Raleigh, any beast

SEVERAL (*cont.*)
will grow fat, if you take
him from the common, and
graze him in the several'
(Johnson; cf. *Sh. Eng.* I,
382–3, 348); 2. 1. 221

SHAPE, (*a*) form of any kind,
(*b*) figure, person; 2. 1. 59, 60

SHAPELESS GEAR, 'uncouth
dress' (Hart); 5. 2. 303

SHOP, the organ of generation
(see O.E.D. sb. 3*c*); 4. 3. 57

SHOWS, O.E.D. (sb.¹ 3) quotes
Babington, 1592, 'About
the beginning of May, when
all things flourished and
yeelded show'; 1. 1. 106

SHREWD, mischievous, mali-
cious; 5. 2. 12

SHROW, variant of 'shrew'; 5.
2. 46

SIGHT (in), conspicuously; 5.
2. 136

SIGN, token, badge, or device
(for identification); 5. 2. 469

SIGNIFICANT token (Armado's
word for a letter); 3. 1. 129

SIMPLICITY, folly, silliness; 4.
2. 22; 4. 3. 52; 5. 2. 52

SINGLED, separated; 5. 1. 79

SIR, a title prefixed to the
Christian name of a person
(cf. mod. 'Rev.'); 4. 2. 11

SIRS, the plural could be used of
either sex, cf. *Ant.* 4. 15. 85,
where Cleopatra addresses
Charmian and Iras as 'good
sirs'; 4. 3. 208

SIT OUT, sc. of the game; 1. 1.
110

SMALL, the part of the leg
below the calf; 5. 2. 639

SMOCK, women's undergar-
ment, shift, chemise; 5. 2.
479

SMOKE, exhalation. Metaphor
= verbiage, idle words; 3. 1.
62

SNEAPING, nipping; 1. 1. 100

SNIP, a snatch; 3. 1. 21

SNUFF (take in), take offence
at; 5. 2. 22

SOD, past participle of 'seethe'
= boil to a decoction; 4. 2.
23

SOLA! hallo! (cf. *M. of V.* 5. 1.
39); 4. 1. 148

SOLACE, provide amusement;
4. 3. 374

SONNET, used loosely of any
short poem of an amatory
character (cf. *ode*); 1. 2. 176;
4. 3. 15, 97, 131

SORE, SOREL, see *buck*; 4. 2. 57
etc.

SORTED, associated with; 1. 1.
253

SOWED COCKLE, etc. Cf. Tilley,
Prov. T 228 'He that sows
thistles shall reap thorns';
4. 3. 380

SPECIALTY, 'a special contract,
obligation, or bond, ex-
pressed in an instrument
under seal' (O.E.D.); 2. 1.
162

SPIRITS, 'the nimble spirits in
the arteries' (cf. *arteries*).
'It was formerly supposed
that certain subtle highly-
refined substances or fluids
(distinguished as natural,
animal, and vital) permeated
the blood and chief organs
of the body' (O.E.D.); 4. 3.
302

SPLEEN, fit, outburst; 5. 2.
117

SPRUCE, dandified, affected; 5.
1. 14; 5. 2. 407

SPUR, with a quibble on 'speer' which was commonly spelt 'spur' at this time (see O.E.D.), and meant, of course, to ask questions. The form was current in S. English, cf. J. Rainoldes, *Overthrow of Stage-Playes* (1593), 'You were disposed to spurre him idle questions'; 2. 1. 117

SQUARE, i.e. the carpenter's setsquare; 'know her foot by the square' = know the length of her foot; 5. 2. 474

STAFF, stave, verse or stanza; 4. 2. 110

STAND, a sheltered position or covert for shooting at game (cf. *M.W.W.* 5. 5. 226; *Sh. Eng.* II, 386); 4. 1. 10

STANZE, old form of 'stanza'; 4. 2. 110

STAPLE, the fibre of wool from which the yarn is spun; 5. 1. 17

STATE, (i) posture, pose; 4. 3. 182; (ii) dignity; 4. 3. 289; (iii) (a) health, (b) property, estate; 5. 2. 425

STATUTE-CAPS, prentice-caps. Hart discovered the statute referred to in regulations 'for the Apparel of London Apprentices', enacted in 1582 by the Lord Mayor and Council, and decreeing 'that from henceforth no Apprentice should presume.... to wear any hat within the City and liberty thereof but a woollen cap, without any silk in or about the same'; 5. 2. 281

STAY THANKSGIVING, wait for the grace at the end; 2. 1. 191

STEEP-UP, precipitous, perpendicular (see note); 4. 1. 2

STILL, always, for ever; 4. 3. 294

STOMACH, 'with a full s.' = (a) well-fed, (b) courageously; 1. 2. 143

STOPS, obstructions, hindrances; 1. 1. 70

STOPPED, deaf; 4. 3. 333

STRAIGHT, at once; 5. 2. 483

STRAIN, tendency; 5. 2. 756

STRANGE, we presume Nathaniel means 'original' or 'startling'; 5. 1. 6

STRAY, cause to stray or wander (cf. O.E.D. 4 c); 5. 2. 759

STUDY, meditate, ponder; 5. 2. 833

SUDDENLY, immediately; 2. 1. 110

SUE, 'how can this be true.... being those that sue', i.e. 'how can those be liable to forfeiture that begin the process? The jest lies in the ambiguity of "sue", which signifies "to prosecute by law," or "to offer a petition"' (Johnson); 5. 2. 427

SUGGEST, prompt, tempt; 5. 2. 766

SUGGESTION, temptation; 1. 1. 158

SUIT, 'out of all suit' = surpassingly; 5. 2. 275

SUITOR, possibly = shooter; 4. 1. 107

SUN, 'get the sun of' = to get on the sunward side of an enemy so that the sun shines in his eyes (O.E.D.). There

SUN (*cont.*)
is also a 'gloze' on 'getting sons' (cf. *Tit.* 2. 3. 21); 4. 3. 366

SUP (trans. vb.), provide supper for; 5. 2. 690

SUPERSCRIPT, superscription, address; 4. 2. 137

SUPERVIZE, look over [Hol.'s word]; 4. 2. 127

SWEAR OUT, forswear, abjure (cf. *outswear*); 2. 1. 103

TABLE-BOOK, note book (cf. *Ham.* 1. 5. 107 'my tables'); 5. 1. 15

TABLES, backgammon; 5. 2. 326

TAFFETA, thin silken stuff of lustrous appearance, from which masks and vizards were made; 5. 2. 159, 406

TAKE A BUTTON-HOLE LOWER, (*a*) help undress, (*b*) 'take down a peg'; 5. 2. 698

TALE, talk, remark; 2. 1. 74

TALENT, a common sixteenth-cent. form of 'talon'; 4. 2. 69

TALK APACE, chatter; 5. 2. 369

TASK (vb.), impose a task upon, give a lesson to; 5. 2. 126

TAWNY, dark-skinned; 1. 1. 173

TEEN, sorrow; 4. 3. 161

TEXT B, The 'text hand' was one of the more elaborate and formal of the various Elizabethan scripts. The 'black' Rosaline is apparently likened to a text B because this letter would require more ink for its formation than any other in the alphabet; 5. 2. 42

THEFT ? Abs. for concrete thieves; 4. 3. 333

THIN-BELLY DOUBLET, 'a doublet with an unpadded belly or lower part' (Onions), as opposed to the 'great-belly doublet' (cf. *Hen. V*, 4. 7. 52). Doubtless Moth is also stressing the leanness of Armado's frame (see *clean-timbered*); 3. 1. 18

THRASONICAL, boastful (Thraso is the braggart in Terence); 5. 1. 12

THREE-PILED, i.e. with a very thick pile, like the richest kind of velvet; 5. 2. 407

THROW UPON, bestow upon; 1. 1. 30

THUMP, Moth's imitation of the noise of a cannon; 3. 1. 64

TIMBERED, see *clean-timbered*; 5. 2. 636

TIME, opportunity, occasion (cf. *Temp.* 2. 1. 299 'conspiracy his time doth take'); 4. 3. 378

TIMON, i.e. scorner of the world, especially of woman; 4. 3. 167

TIRED, (*a*) incorrigibly lazy (O.E.D.); (*b*) lit. attired, hence = harnessed; 4. 2. 133

TOIL, snare, net; 4. 3. 3

TOOTHDRAWER, see *brooch*; 5. 2. 617

TOUCH, hit or stroke in fencing; 5. 1. 56

TOY (sb.), trifle; 4. 3. 167, 197

TRAIN, entice; 1. 1. 71

TRANSLATION OF, 'commentary upon' (Schmidt); 5. 2. 51

TRENCHER-KNIGHT, one who serves ladies at table (cf. 'carpet-knight' and l. 477 below); 5. 2. 464

TREY, throw of three in dice-play; 5. 2. 232

TROYAN, good fellow, boon companion, dissolute fellow (cf. *1 Hen. IV*, 2. 1. 77); 5. 2. 634, 673

TRUE, honest; 1. 1. 302; 4. 3. 185, 209

TUMBLER'S HOOP, a hoop garnished with ribbons, with which the tumbler did his tricks and which he wore across his body like a corporal's scarf; 3. 1. 187

TURN, (vb.), shape, fashion; 1. 2. 176; Costard mistakenly says 'turn off '—like a hangman; 5. 2. 508

TURTLE, turtle-dove; 5. 2. 901, i.e. simple lover; 4. 3. 507

TWICE-SOD SIMPLICITY, quintessence of stupidity; (cf. *sod*) 4. 2. 23

TYBURN, 'the shape of Love's Tyburn' (see *corner-cap*). Cf. Lyly, *Pappe with a Hatchett*, 1589 (Bond, III, 401), 'Theres one with a lame wit, which will not weare a foure cornered cap, then let him put on Tiburne, that hath but three corners.' It is difficult to believe that Lyly's words did not suggest Shakespeare's; 4. 3. 52

UNCASE, undress; 5. 2. 596

UNCONFIRMED, inexperienced (cf. *Ado* 3. 1. 114); 4. 2. 18

UNDO, untie, release; 5. 2. 425

UNSEEMING, not seeming willing; 2. 1. 153

UNUM CITA, take one example; 5. 1. 65

UPSHOOT, a term of archery = 'the best shot up to any point in the contest' (*Sh. Eng.* II, 383); 4. 1. 135

USURPING, false; 4. 3. 255

UTTER, (*a*) speak, (*b*) offer for sale; 2. 1. 16

VAILING, lowering, letting fall (naut. term, cf. 'vailing her high-top', *M. of V.* 1. 1. 28); 5. 2. 297

VARA, dial. = very; 5. 2. 487

VARNISH, lend freshness to; 4. 3. 240

VARY, alter, change; 4. 3. 97

VASSAL, abject creature; 1. 1. 249

VEAL! Fourfold quibble, (*a*) German pron. of 'well!' = excellent, (*b*) veil = mask, (*c*) calf, (*d*) last syllable of 'Longaville'; 5. 2. 247

VENETIA, VENETIA, CHI NON TI VEDE, NON TI PRETIA, a tag of Italian phrase found in Florio's *First Fruites* (1578), and other Elizabethan books: 'Venice, Venice, who seeth thee not, praiseth thee not,'; 4. 2. 102–3

VENEW, a thrust or stroke in fencing; 5. 1. 56

VENTRICLE, 'The ventricle of memory—*ventriculus* or *cellula memorativa*—in medieval nomenclature was the third ventricle of the brain, the first and second being

VENTRICLE (*cont.*)
the seat of imagination and
reason' (*Sh. Eng.* 1, 421);
4. 2. 75

VIA, 'an adverb of encouraging
much used by commanders,
as also by riders to their
horses' (Florio); 5. 1. 144

VIDEO, ET GAUDEO, I see and
rejoice; 5. 1. 31

VIDESNE QUIS VENIT Lat. 'Do
you see who comes?'; 5. 1.
30

VIR SAPIT QUI PAUCA LOQUITUR,
a phrase from Lyly's *Grammar*, 'the Relative agreeth
with his Antecedent in Gen-
der, Number and Person, as
Vir sapit etc. That man is
wise that speaketh few
things or words'; 4. 2.
83

VISITED, plague-stricken; 5. 2.
422

VISOR, VIZARD, mask; 5. 2. 227,
etc.

VOLABLE, quick (Armado's
speech); 3. 1. 65

WAIT, attend upon; 5. 2. 401

WAKE, village feast (lit. an all-
night vigil previous to the
annual feast of the dedica-
tion of the village church);
5. 2. 318

WARD, guard; 3. 1. 131

WASSAIL, revelry, carouse; 5.
2. 318

WAX, increase (with a quibble
upon 'sealing-wax'); 5. 2.
10

WEEDING, i.e. what has been
weeded; 1. 1. 96

WEEDS, dress, clothes; 5. 2.
797

WEEK, 'in by th' week' =
trapped, caught. The origin
and literal meaning of the
phrase are unknown; 5. 2.
274

WEEPING-RIPE, ready to weep;
5. 2. 61

WEIGH, (*a*) to be of the same
weight as, (*b*) to value at a
certain rate; 5. 2. 26, 27

WELKIN, heaven; 1. 1. 217

WELL ADVISED, in one's right
mind (cf. *Errors*, 3. 2. 213);
5. 2. 434

WELL-LIKING, in good condition, plump; 5. 2. 268

WHALE BONE (white as), a proverbial phrase, often found
in early English poetry; 5. 2.
332

WHAT TIME O' DAY? when may
that be?; 2. 1. 120

WHIRLS, metaphor from Fortune's wheel (Schmidt); 4.
3. 381

WHITELY, pale; 3. 1. 195

WIDE O' THE BOW HAND, i.e.
wide of the mark (lit. wide
on the left or bow-hand side
of the target. The exclamation might be called out
from the butts to the archers
by the 'direction-giver', see
Two Gent. G.); 4. 1. 132

WILL, intention; 2. 1. 49;
'by my will' intentionally;
2. 1. 98

WIMPLED, muffled, blindfol-
ded; 3. 1. 178

WINK, close the eyes; 1. 1.
43

WIT-OLD, (*a*) feeble-witted,
(*b*) quibble upon 'wittol' =
a contented cuckold; 5. 1.
59

WOODCOCK, a type of stupidity; hence, a fool; 4. 3. 80

WOOLWARD, with woollen clothing next the skin; 5. 2. 708

WORKING, operation, effect; 1. 2. 9

WORM, used as an expression of pity, especially for those in love (cf. *Temp.* 3. 1. 31 'Poor worm, thou art infected'); 4. 3. 151

WORT, sweet unfermented beer; 5. 2. 233

WORTHY, excellence (cf. *Two Gent.* 2. 4. 164 'her whose worth makes other worthies nothing'); 4. 3. 232; 'Nine Worthies' (q.v.) 5. 1. 113

YARD, membrum virile; 5. 2. 667

YCLIPED, called (deliberately archaic); 1. 1. 237; 5. 2. 594

YEA AND NAY (by), a Puritan expletive, which Berowne uses jocularly; 1. 1. 54

YEARS, 'in y.'—into wrinkles; 5. 2. 465

ZANY, a stage-buffoon who imitated the tricks of the principal clown or fool; 5. 2. 463

ZEALOUS, fervent; 5. 2. 116

WORDSWORTH CLASSICS

General Editors: Marcus Clapham & Clive Reynard

JANE AUSTEN
Emma
Mansfield Park
Northanger Abbey
Persuasion
Pride and Prejudice
Sense and Sensibility

ARNOLD BENNETT
Anna of the Five Towns

R. D. BLACKMORE
Lorna Doone

ANNE BRONTË
Agnes Grey
The Tenant of
Wildfell Hall

CHARLOTTE BRONTË
Jane Eyre
The Professor
Shirley
Villette

EMILY BRONTË
Wuthering Heights

JOHN BUCHAN
Greenmantle
Mr Standfast
The Thirty-Nine Steps

SAMUEL BUTLER
The Way of All Flesh

LEWIS CARROLL
Alice in Wonderland

CERVANTES
Don Quixote

G. K. CHESTERTON
Father Brown:
Selected Stories
The Man who was
Thursday

ERSKINE CHILDERS
The Riddle of the Sands

JOHN CLELAND
Memoirs of a Woman of
Pleasure: Fanny Hill

WILKIE COLLINS
The Moonstone
The Woman in White

JOSEPH CONRAD
Heart of Darkness
Lord Jim
The Secret Agent

J. FENIMORE COOPER
The Last of the
Mohicans

STEPHEN CRANE
The Red Badge of
Courage

THOMAS DE QUINCEY
Confessions of an English
Opium Eater

DANIEL DEFOE
Moll Flanders
Robinson Crusoe

CHARLES DICKENS
Bleak House
David Copperfield
Great Expectations
Hard Times
Little Dorrit
Martin Chuzzlewit
Oliver Twist
Pickwick Papers
A Tale of Two Cities

BENJAMIN DISRAELI
Sybil

THEODOR DOSTOEVSKY
Crime and Punishment

SIR ARTHUR CONAN
DOYLE
The Adventures of
Sherlock Holmes
The Case-Book of
Sherlock Holmes
The Lost World &
Other Stories
The Return of
Sherlock Holmes
Sir Nigel

GEORGE DU MAURIER
Trilby

ALEXANDRE DUMAS
The Three Musketeers

MARIA EDGEWORTH
Castle Rackrent

GEORGE ELIOT
The Mill on the Floss
Middlemarch
Silas Marner

HENRY FIELDING
Tom Jones

F. SCOTT FITZGERALD
A Diamond as Big as the
Ritz & Other Stories
The Great Gatsby
Tender is the Night

GUSTAVE FLAUBERT
Madame Bovary

JOHN GALSWORTHY
In Chancery
The Man of Property
To Let

ELIZABETH GASKELL
Cranford
North and South

KENNETH GRAHAME
The Wind in the
Willows

GEORGE & WEEDON
GROSSMITH
Diary of a Nobody

RIDER HAGGARD
She

THOMAS HARDY
Far from the
Madding Crowd
The Mayor of Casterbridge
The Return of the
Native
Tess of the d'Urbervilles
The Trumpet Major
Under the Greenwood
Tree

NATHANIEL
HAWTHORNE
The Scarlet Letter

O. HENRY
Selected Stories

HOMER
The Iliad
The Odyssey

E. W. HORNUNG
Raffles: The Amateur
Cracksman

VICTOR HUGO
The Hunchback of
Notre Dame
Les Misérables: volume 1
Les Misérables: volume 2

HENRY JAMES
The Ambassadors
Daisy Miller & Other
Stories
The Golden Bowl
The Turn of the Screw
& The Aspern Papers

M. R. JAMES
Ghost Stories

JEROME K. JEROME
Three Men in a Boat

JAMES JOYCE
Dubliners
A Portrait of the Artist
as a Young Man

RUDYARD KIPLING
Captains Courageous
Kim
The Man who would be
King & Other Stories
Plain Tales from the
Hills

D. H. LAWRENCE
The Rainbow
Sons and Lovers
Women in Love

SHERIDAN LE FANU
(edited by M. R. James)
Madam Crowl's Ghost
& Other Stories

JACK LONDON
Call of the Wild &
White Fang

HERMAN MELVILLE
Moby Dick
Typee

H. H. MUNRO
The Complete Stories of
Saki

EDGAR ALLAN POE
Tales of Mystery and
Imagination

FREDERICK ROLFE
Hadrian the Seventh

SIR WALTER SCOTT
Ivanhoe

WILLIAM
SHAKESPEARE
All's Well that Ends
Well
Antony and Cleopatra
As You Like It
A Comedy of Errors
Hamlet
Henry IV Part 1
Henry IV part 2
Henry V
Julius Caesar
King Lear
Macbeth
Measure for Measure
The Merchant of Venice
A Midsummer Night's
Dream
Othello
Richard II
Richard III
Romeo and Juliet
The Taming of the
Shrew
The Tempest
Troilus and Cressida
Twelfth Night
A Winter's Tale

MARY SHELLEY
Frankenstein

ROBERT LOUIS
STEVENSON
Dr Jekyll and Mr Hyde

BRAM STOKER
Dracula

JONATHAN SWIFT
Gulliver's Travels

W. M. THACKERAY
Vanity Fair

TOLSTOY
War and Peace

ANTHONY TROLLOPE
Barchester Towers
Dr Thorne
Framley Parsonage
The Last Chronicle of
Barset
The Small House at
Allington
The Warden

MARK TWAIN
Tom Sawyer &
Huckleberry Finn

JULES VERNE
Around the World in 80
Days &
Five Weeks in a Balloon
20,000 Leagues Under
the Sea

VOLTAIRE
Candide

EDITH WHARTON
The Age of Innocence

OSCAR WILDE
Lord Arthur Savile's
Crime & Other Stories
The Picture of Dorian
Gray

VIRGINIA WOOLF
Orlando
To the Lighthouse

P. C. WREN
Beau Geste

DISTRIBUTION

**AUSTRALIA, BRUNEI
& MALAYSIA
Reed Editions**
22 Salmon Street, Port Melbourne
Vic 3207, Australia
Tel: (03) 245 7111
Fax (03) 245 7333

**CZECH REPUBLIC
Bohemian Ventures spol s r o**
Delnicka 13
170 00 Prague 7
Tel: 02 877837 Fax: 02 801498

**DENMARK
BOG-FAN**
St. Kongensgade 65
DK-1264 København K

**FRANCE
Bookking International**
60 Rue Saint-André-des-Arts
75006 Paris

**GERMANY, AUSTRIA
& SWITZERLAND
Swan Buch-Marketing GmbH**
Goldscheuerstrabe 16
D-7640 Kehl Am Rhein, Germany

**GREAT BRITAIN & IRELAND
Wordsworth Editions Ltd**
Cumberland House, Crib Street,
Ware, Hertfordshire SG12 9ET

Selecta Books
The Selectabook
Distribution Centre
Folly Road, Roundway, Devizes
Wiltshire SN10 2HR

**SCOTLAND
Lomond Books**
36 West Shore Road, Granton,
Edinburgh EH5 1QD

**INDIA
OM Book Service**
1690 First Floor
Nai Sarak, Delhi – 110006
Tel: 3279823-3265303 Fax: 3278091

**IRAN
World Book Distributors**
No 26 Behrooz Street, Suit 6
Tehran 19119
Tel: 9821 8714622 Fax: 9871 50044

**ISRAEL
Timmy Marketing Limited**
Israel Ben Zeev 12
Ramot Gimmel, Jerusalem
Tel: 02-865266 Fax: 02-880035

**ITALY
Magis Books SRL**
Via Raffaello 31/C
Zona Ind Mancasale, 42100 Reggio Emilia
Tel: 0522-920999 Fax: 0522-920666

**PHILIPPINES
I J Sagun Enterprises**
P O Box 4322 CPO Manila
2 Topaz Road, Greenheights Village
Taytay, Rizal Tel: 631-80-61 TO 66

**PORTUGAL
International Publishing Services Ltd**
Rua da Cruz da Carreira, 4B,1100 Lisboa
Tel: 01-570051 Fax: 01-3522066

**SINGAPORE
Book Station**
18 Leo Drive, Singapore
Tel: 4511998 Fax: 4529188

**SLOVAK REPUBLIC
Slovak Ventures spol s r o**
Stefanikova 128, 94901 Nitra
Tel/Fax: 087 25105

**CYPRUS
Huckleberry Trading**
4 Isabella, Anavargos, Pafos, Cyprus
Tel: 06-231313

**SOUTH AFRICA
Struik Book Distributors (Pty) Ltd**
Graph Avenue, Montague Gardens,
7441 P O Box 193 Maitland 7405
South Africa
Tel: (021) 551-5900 Fax: (021) 551-1124

**SPAIN
Ribera Libros, S.L.**
Poligono Martiartu, Calle 1 – no 6
48480 Arrigorriaga, Vizcaya
Tel: 34-4-6713607 (Almacen)
34-4-4418787 (Libreria)
Fax: 34-4-6713608 (Almacen)
34-4-4418029 (Libreria)

**USA, CANADA & MEXICO
Universal Sales & Marketing**
230 Fifth Avenue, Suite 1212
New York, N Y 10001 USA
Tel: 212-481-3500 Fax: 212-481-3534

DIRECT MAIL
Redvers
Redvers House, 13 Fairmile,
Henley-on-Thames, Oxfordshire RG9 2JR
Tel: 0491 572656 Fax: 0491 573590